Reasoning
Olympiad

Class 03

A must have book for all
Olympiads & Talent Search Exams...

by
Ruchika

BLOOM CAP
Bloom Cap Edu Ventures Pvt. Ltd.

Bloom Cap Edu Ventures Pvt. Ltd.

卐 **Administrative & Production Office**

'Ramchhaya' 4577/15, Agarwal Road, Darya Ganj, New Delhi -110002
Tele: 011- 47630600, 43518550

卐 **ISBN :** 978-93-25519-02-2

卐 **PRICE :** ₹100.00

卐 **PO No :** TXT-XX-XXXXXXX-X-XX

For further information about the books log on to
www.bloomcap.org

Follow us on   

Preface

"Future belongs to those Who prepares for it today"

School Olympiads are National & International level competitions conducted by different Government, Non-Government & Educational Organisations with the purpose of making the children ready to face competitive exams. The challenging Questions asked in Olympiads motivate them to learn more & more and bring out the best result with improved academic performance. The Awards & Scholarship offered by Olympiads motivate children to aspire & strive for doing better and emerge out to be the best.

Reasoning Olympiads

Reasoning or Logical thinking is the ability of mind that helps in dealing with complex situations. It is also directly related to evolving careers like Software Development, Coding, Mobile App Development etc.

Reasoning Olympiads are targeted to induce & enhance the logical thinking skills and Analytical Approach in students which further aid to improve their academics.

'Bloom Reasoning Olympiad Study Book Class 3' is a perfect resource to Study & Practice for Olympiad Exams and other National & State Level Talent Search Exams & Other Competitions.

Some Special Features of Bloom Reasoning Olympiad Study Books are;

- Complete coverage of all the aspects of Reasoning; Verbal, Non-Verbal, Analytical & Logical Reasoning etc.
- Chapterwise Exercises having different types of Objective Questions at par with the Olympiad Level.
- Detailed Explanation for each question.
- Olympiad Pattern Practice Sets at the end.

This book is prepared by Expert Panel with the utmost care, still if you have any suggestions regarding its improvement then feel free to contact us at olympiads@bloomcap.org. We will try to inculcate your suggestions in the further editions.

Contents

Matching Pairs

'Matching Pairs' as the name suggests means similarity between the elements in the first pair and the elements in the second pair. Students are required to find the similarity between them and complete the second pair in the same way as the first pair.

EXAMPLE 1 Identify the relation between the objects in the first pair and then find the object that will replace the question mark.

   (a)   (b)   (c)   (d)

Sol. (c) As fishes are kept in aquarium. Similarly, flowers are kept in flower pot. Hence, option (c) is correct.

Directions (Ex. Nos. 2-4) Two numbers/letters written in the arrow are related to each other. Find the missing term in the second arrow following the same rule.

EXAMPLE 2

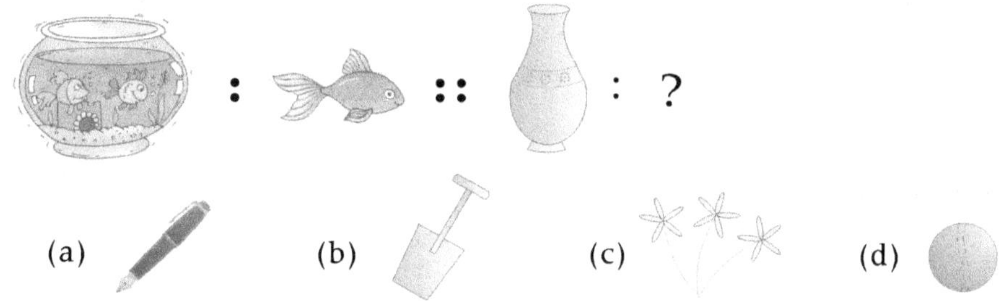

   (a) 36   (b) 27   (c) 45   (d) 35

Sol. (a) As, $6 \times 4 = 24$, similarly $9 \times 4 = 36$. So, the missing number is 36. Hence, option (a) is correct.

EXAMPLE 3

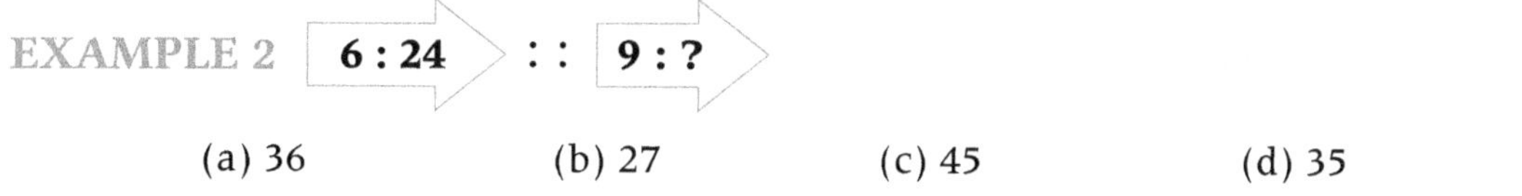

   (a) G   (b) U   (c) S   (d) Z

Sol. (c) As, 'D' is fourth letter from the starting in the English alphabet and 'W' is fourth letter from the end. Similarly, 'H' is eighth letter from the starting and 'S' is eighth letter from the end. So, 'S' is the missing letter. Hence, option (c) is correct.

Following table showing letters position in English alphabetical series will help the students to solve these type of questions.

Alphabet	A	B	C	D	E	F	G	H	I	J	K	L	M	N	O	P	Q	R	S	T	U	V	W	X	Y	Z
Position	1	2	3	4	5	6	7	8	9	10	11	12	13	14	15	16	17	18	19	20	21	22	23	24	25	26

EXAMPLE 4   TRAIN : RAIN   : :   PAGE : ?

(a) GEA   (b) AGE   (c) GAP   (d) PAG

Sol. (b) The first letter of the word TRAIN is removed to get the word RAIN. Similarly, the first letter of the word PAGE is to be removed to get the AGE. Hence, option (b) is correct.

⏰ Let's Practice

1. Find the picture which will complete the second pair in the same way as the first pair.

(a)   (b)   (c)   (d)

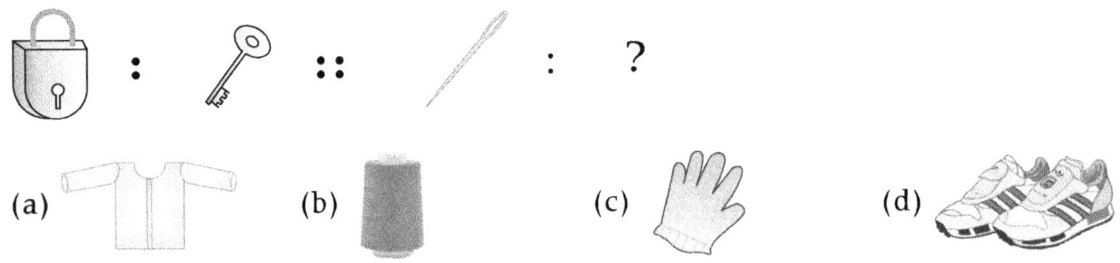

2. Complete the second pair in the same way as the first pair.

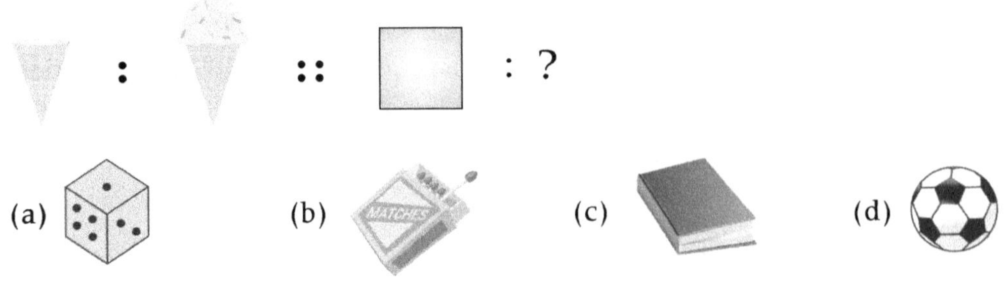

(a)   (b)   (c)   (d)

3. Which pattern from the given options will complete the second pair in the same way as the first the pair?

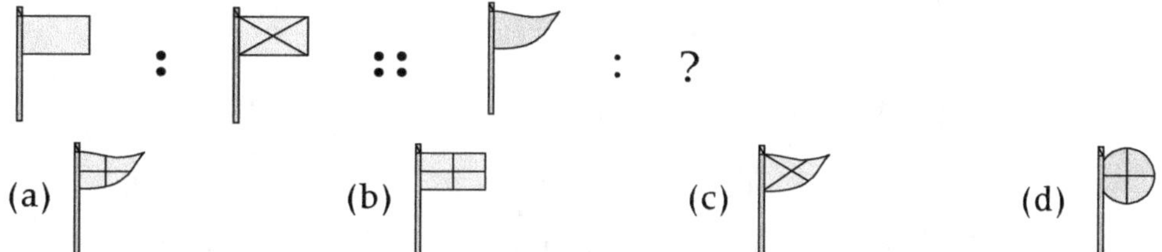

(a)   (b)   (c)   (d)

4. Look at the given figures carefully, then identify the relation between the first two figures and find the missing figure.

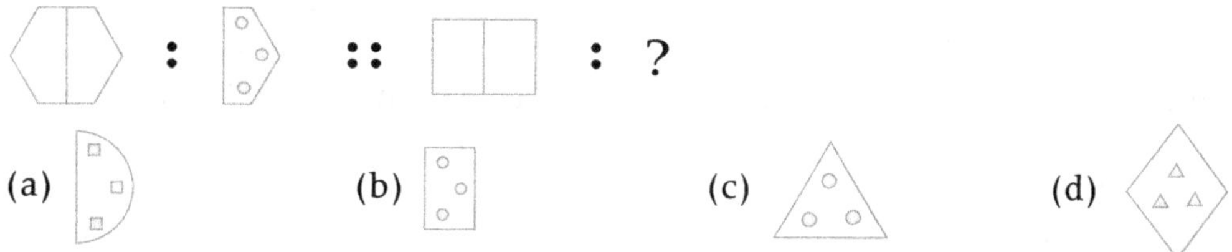

(a)   (b)   (c)   (d)

5. Which pattern will complete the second pair in the same way as the first pair?

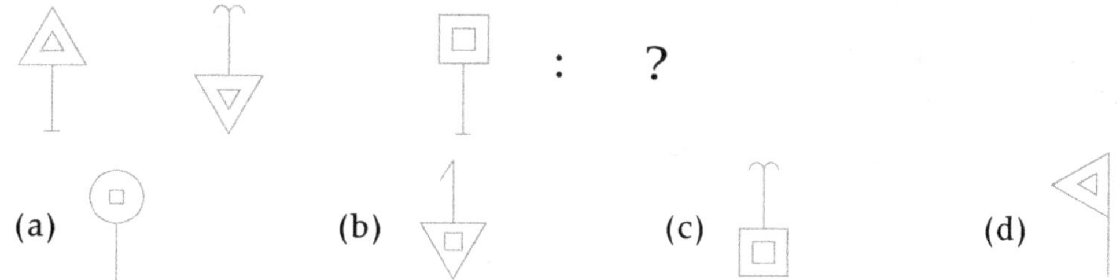

(a)   (b)   (c)   (d)

6. The numbers written on the first and second balloons are related to each other in a certain way. Find the number that should be written in the fourth balloon following the same pattern which first two follow.

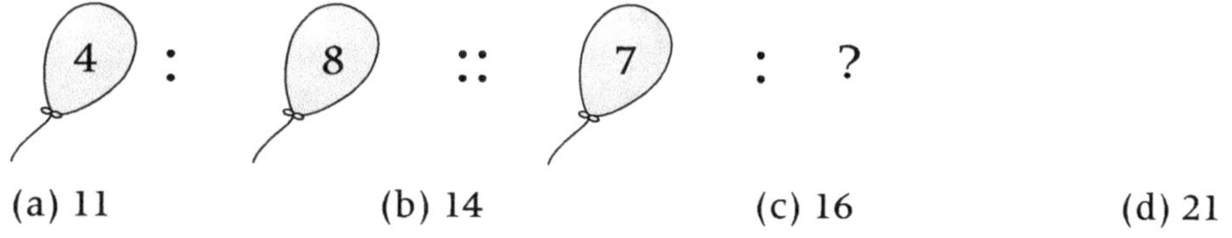

(a) 11   (b) 14   (c) 16   (d) 21

7. Ice-cream prices are shown on the ice-creams. First two are related to each other. Find the price of fourth ice-cream following the pattern which first two follow.

(a) ₹ 40   (b) ₹ 60   (c) ₹ 55   (d) ₹ 45

Directions (Q. Nos. 8-10) In these questions, the numbers/letters are linked in some way. Identify the relation which will come in place of question mark.

8. 58 : 29 :: 86 : ?

(a) 40   (b) 43   (c) 44   (d) 42

9. MN : NM :: OQ : ?

(a) QO   (b) OQ   (c) MO   (d) OM

10. C : Cat :: N : ?

(a) Nose   (b) Neck   (c) Nice   (d) Net

11. Some letters shown below in each box are related to each other. Find the missing letter.

PQ : R :: DE : ?

(a) T   (b) M   (c) G   (d) F

12. Letters given below are linked to each other in the pair. Identify the relation and then find the missing letters.

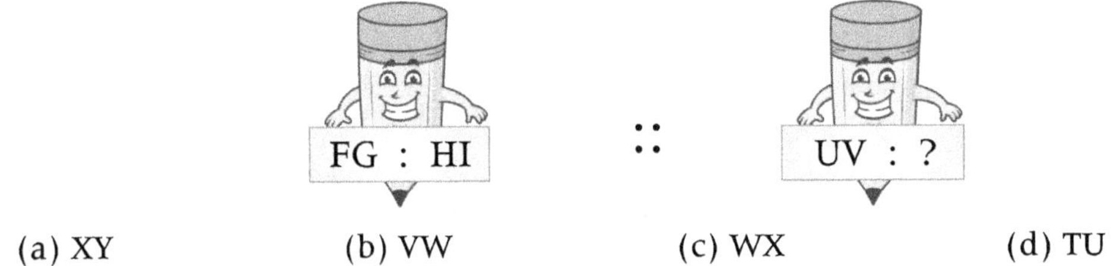

(a) XY   (b) VW   (c) WX   (d) TU

13. Some letters are written on the toffees shown below. Identify the relation between the letters on the first toffee and then find the missing letters.

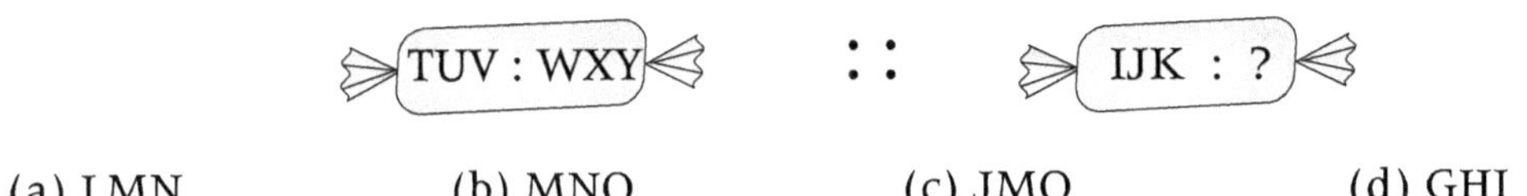

(a) LMN   (b) MNO   (c) JMO   (d) GHI

14. Identify the relation between the given pairs and find the missing term.

(a) N13   (b) M14   (c) M13   (d) N14

15. Day is to Sun, as Night is to ?

    (a) Bulb
    (b) Moon
    (c) Dark
    (d) Sleep

16. Tongue is to Taste, as Ears is to ?

    (a) Sense
    (b) Feel
    (c) Look
    (d) Hear

17. Bird is to Sky, as Duck is to ?

    (a) Water
    (b) Swim
    (c) Quack
    (d) Fly

18. What should come in place of question mark such that the second pair follows the same pattern which first pair follows?

    C-three : E-five :: I-nine : ?

    (a) H-Eight
    (b) J-Ten
    (c) G-Seven
    (d) K-Eleven

19. Triangle is related to three as square is related to ?
    (a) two
    (b) five
    (c) four
    (d) six

20. Mango is to fruit as brinjal is to ?
    (a) bird
    (b) tree
    (c) animal
    (d) vegetable

Chapter 02

Odd One Out

'Odd One Out' means finding a figure/term from the given group of figures/terms, which does not belong to the group.

EXAMPLE 1 From the given alternatives, find which one is different from others.

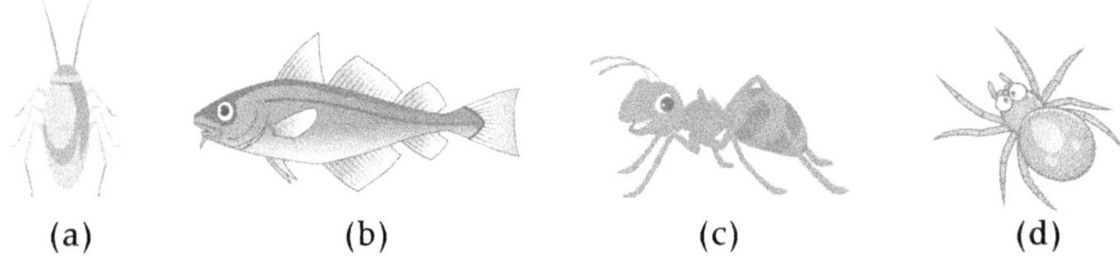

Sol. (b) Beetle, ant and spider are insects and found on land, but fish is an aquatic animal i.e., found under water. So, fish is different from others. Hence, option (b) is correct.

EXAMPLE 2 Identify the one that does not belong to the group.

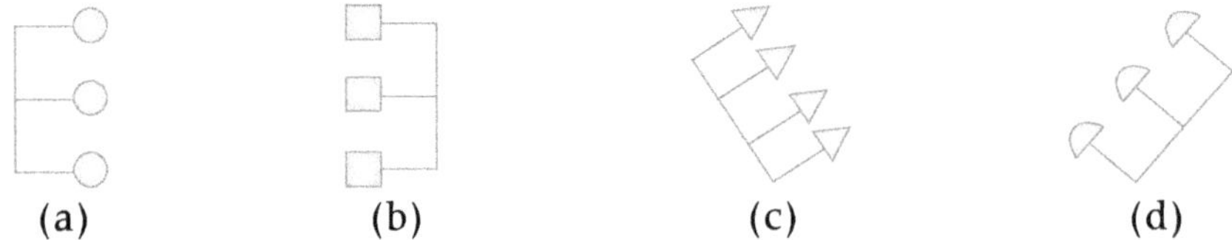

Sol. (c) In figures (a), (b) and (d), the number of shapes attached with lines is three, while in figure (c) it is four. So, figure (c) does not belong to the group. Hence, option (c) is correct.

EXAMPLE 3 Find which number on the chart is different from others.

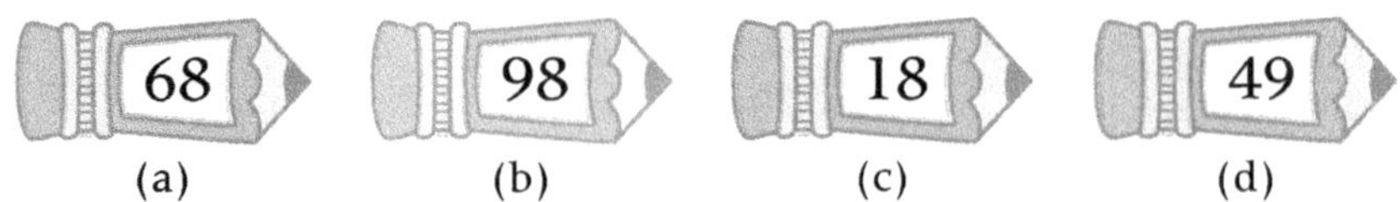

Sol. (d) Except 49, all the numbers are even while 49 is an odd number. Hence, option (d) is correct.

EXAMPLE 4 Which pair of letters does not belong to the group?

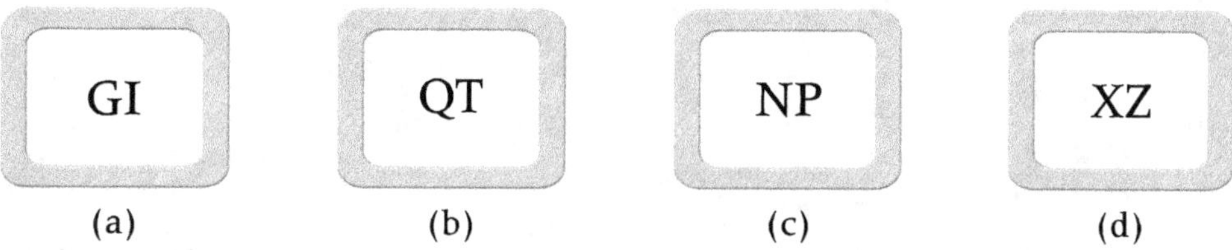

<table>
<tr><td>GI</td><td>QT</td><td>NP</td><td>XZ</td></tr>
<tr><td>(a)</td><td>(b)</td><td>(c)</td><td>(d)</td></tr>
</table>

Sol. (b) The pattern is as follows :

$$G \xrightarrow{H} I, \quad Q \xrightarrow{R, S} T, \quad N \xrightarrow{O} P, \quad X \xrightarrow{Y} Z$$

Here, pair of letters pair 'QT' follows different pattern. So, QT does not belong to the group. Hence, option (b) is correct.

⏰ Let's Practice

1. Following pictures are there on a wall in a classroom. Find a picture, which is different from others.

(a)   (b)   (c)   (d)

2. Among the clocks shown below three are same in a certain way and one is different. Find that clock, which is different from others.

(a)   (b)   (c)   (d)

3. Find which pose of sparrow is different from others.

(a)   (b)   (c)   (d)

4. In a drawing book, following shapes are given. Find that figure, which is different from others in the group.

(a) 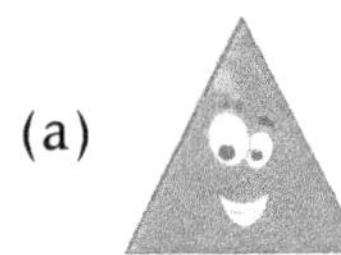   (b)    (c) 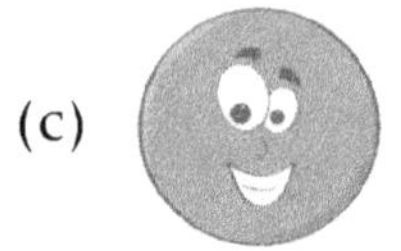   (d) 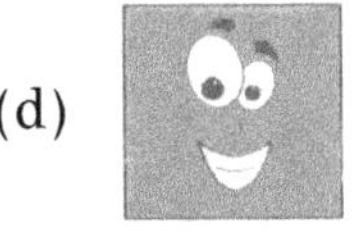

5. A child draw the following shapes in his drawing notebook and keep the one side, which is different from others. Find that shape from the given shapes.

(a) 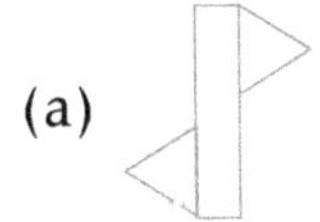   (b) 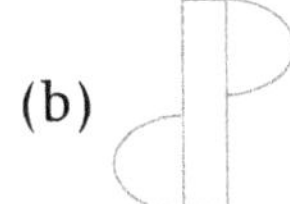   (c)    (d) 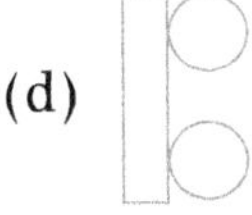

6. Which figure from the given alternatives is different from others in the group?

(a) 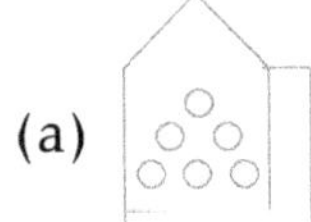   (b) 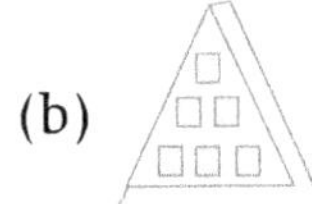   (c) 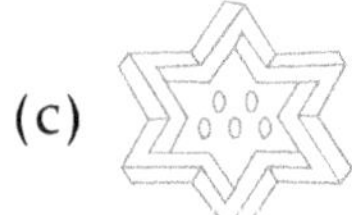   (d) 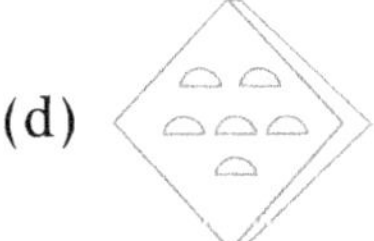

Directions (Q. Nos. 7 and 8) Identify the figure which is different from others.

7. (a) 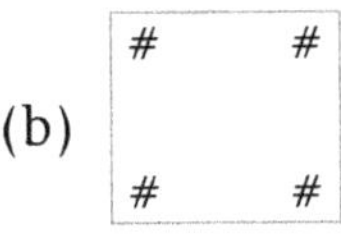   (b) 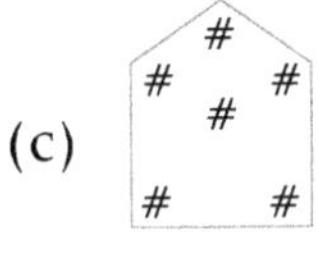   (c) 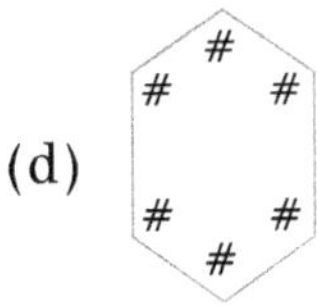   (d) 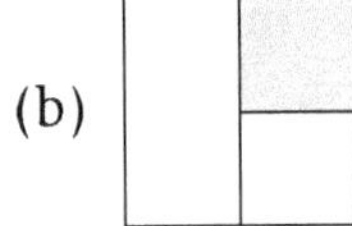

8. (a) 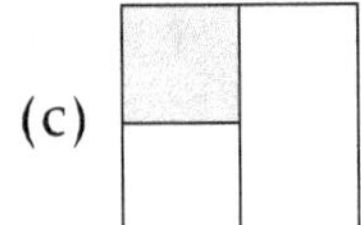   (b) 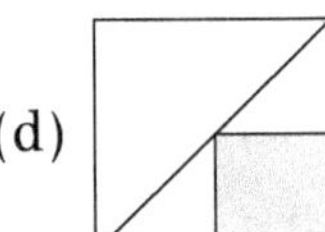   (c) 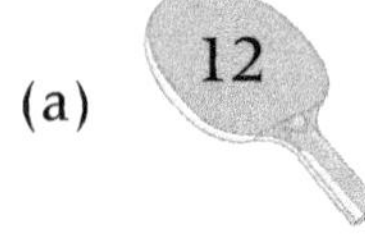   (d) 

9. Bats and their sizes are given. Find the one which is different.

(a) 

   (b)

   (c)

   (d)

10. Which number does not belong to the group?

(a) 528   (b) 809   (c) 924   (d) 621

11. Find a number from the given alternatives which is different in the group.

(a) 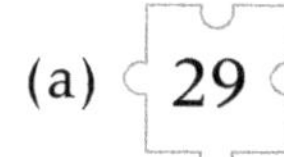 29
(b) 17
(c) 14
(d) 47

12. Find a number from the given alternatives which is different in the group.

(a) 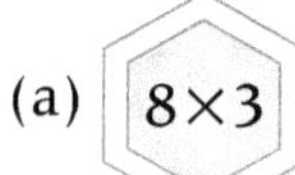 8×3
(b) 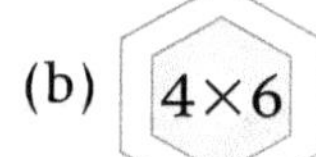 4×6
(c) 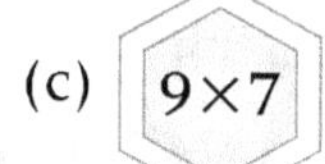 9×7
(d) 12×2

13. Which number does not belong to the group?

(a) 16 ÷ 4
(b) 32 ÷ 8
(c) 28 ÷ 7
(d) 25 ÷ 5

14. Find the letter which is different from others.

(a) 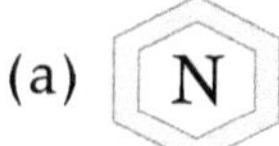 N
(b) 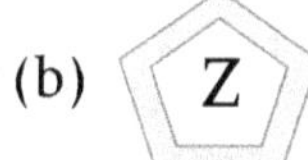 Z
(c)  E
(d) 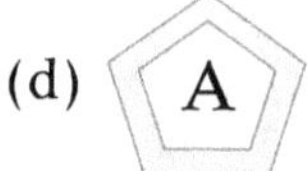 A

15. Which group of letters does not belongs to the group?

(a)  FD
(b)  MK
(c) 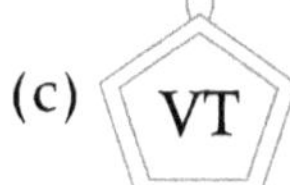 VT
(d) RO

16. Some letters are given in different shapes. Find that group of letters which is different.

(a)  FBF
(b) 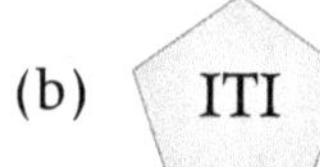 ITI
(c) 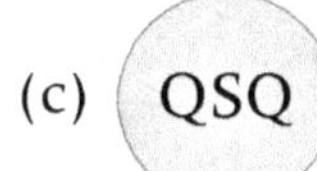 QSQ
(d)  MTN

Directions (Q. Nos. 17 and 18) Identify the group of letters which is different from others.

17. (a) 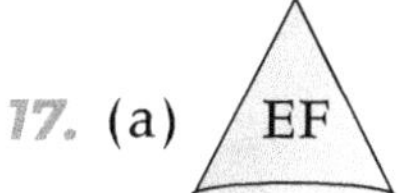 EF
(b) 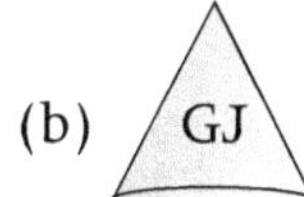 GJ
(c) 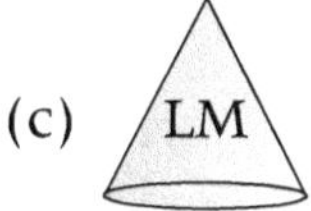 LM
(d) 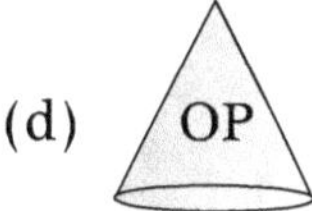 OP

18. (a) PQP
(b) HIJ
(c) WXY
(d) 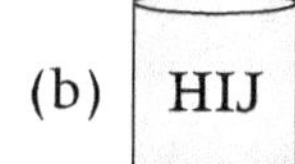 LMN

19. Which one is different from the given alternatives?

(a) 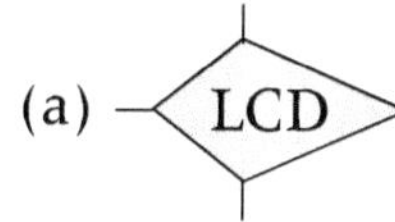 LCD
(b)  Oven
(c)  Truck
(d) 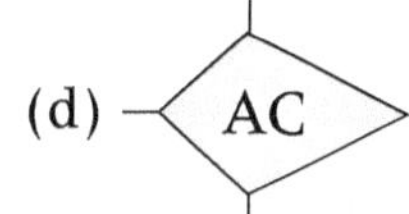 AC

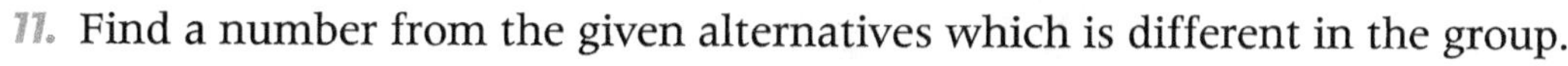

What Comes Next?

In this chapter, questions are asked in which a series consisting of pictures, letters, numbers or patterns is given and it is required to find the term which will continue the series.

EXAMPLE 1 Some pictures are shown below following a certain patterns. Based on that find the missing figure.

(a)   (b)   (c)   (d)

Sol. (b) The first and fifth pictures are same. So, the missing picture should be same as second picture as shown in option (b). Hence, option (b) is correct.

EXAMPLE 2 The ice-creams shown below are grouped in patterns 1, 2 and 3. Find the number of ice-creams in pattern 4.

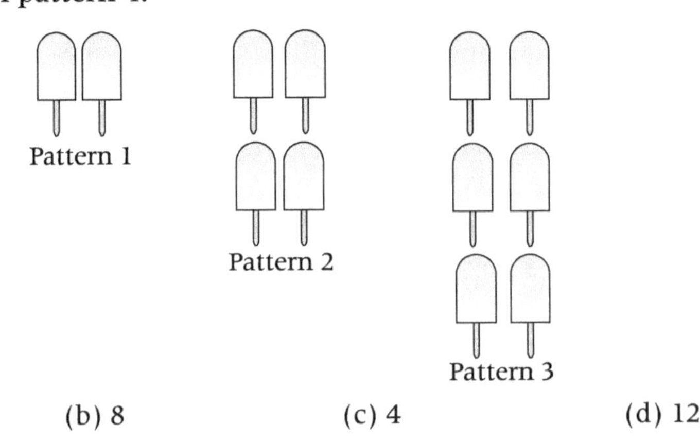

(a) 10   (b) 8   (c) 4   (d) 12

Sol. (b) In pattern 1st, there are 2 ice-creams; in pattern 2nd, there are 4 ice-creams and in pattern 3rd, there are 6 ice-creams. So, the pattern is as follows :

$$2 \xrightarrow{+2} 4 \xrightarrow{+2} 6 \xrightarrow{+2} \boxed{8}$$

Thus, there should be 8 ice-creams in pattern 4. Hence, option (b) is correct.

EXAMPLE 3 The number series is given below. Find the number that will continue the series.

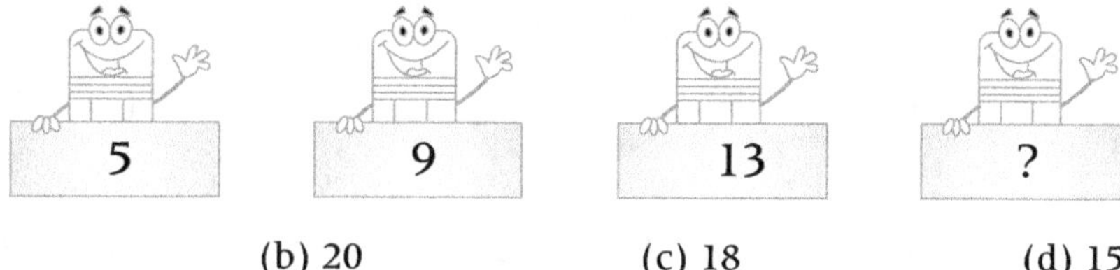

(a) 17	(b) 20	(c) 18	(d) 15

Sol. (a) The pattern is as follows :

$$5 \xrightarrow{+4} 9 \xrightarrow{+4} 13 \xrightarrow{+4} \boxed{17}$$

So, '17' will continue the given series. Hence, option (a) is correct.

EXAMPLE 4 Some ice-cream cups are shown below following a certain pattern. Find the missing letters that should come in place of question mark(?).

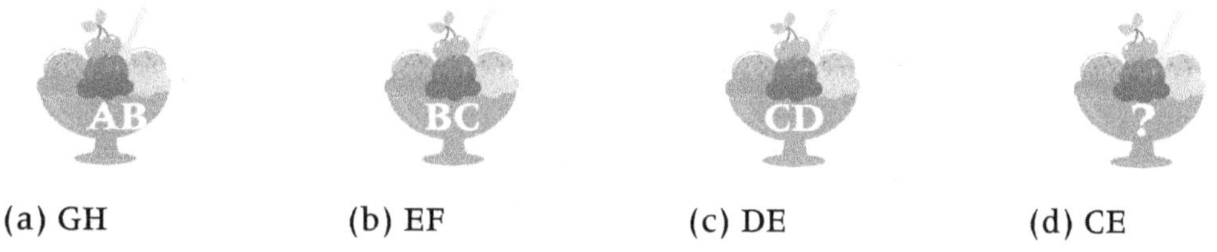

(a) GH	(b) EF	(c) DE	(d) CE

Sol. (c) The pattern is as follows :

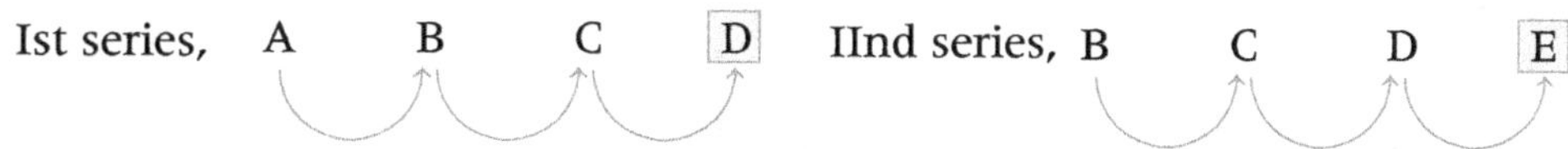

So, 'DE' should come in place of question mark. Hence, option (c) is correct.

1. Which balloon will be the next balloon in the given series?

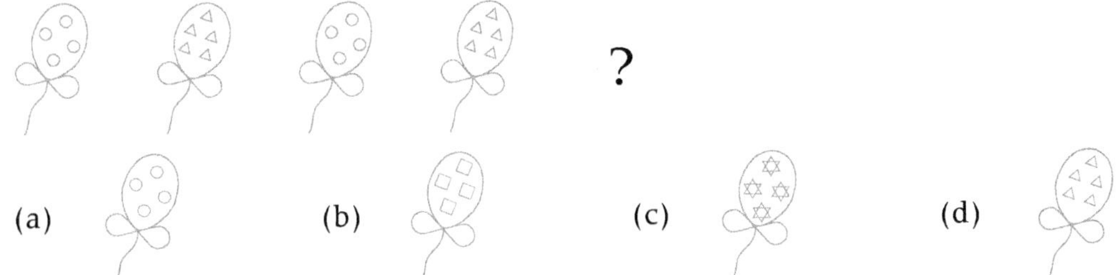

(a)　　　　(b)　　　　(c)　　　　(d)

2. Marie arrange her dolls as follows. Find the doll that will continue the series.

(a)　　　　(b)　　　　(c)　　　　(d)

3. Which pattern from the given alternatives will continue the series?

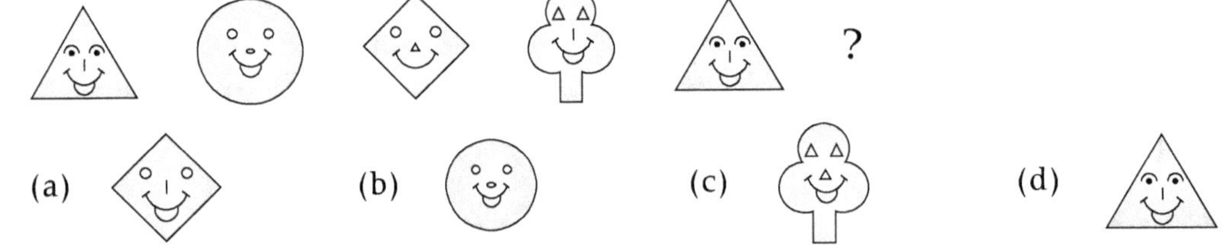

(a)　　　　(b)　　　　(c)　　　　(d)

4. How many teddies will be there in pattern 5?

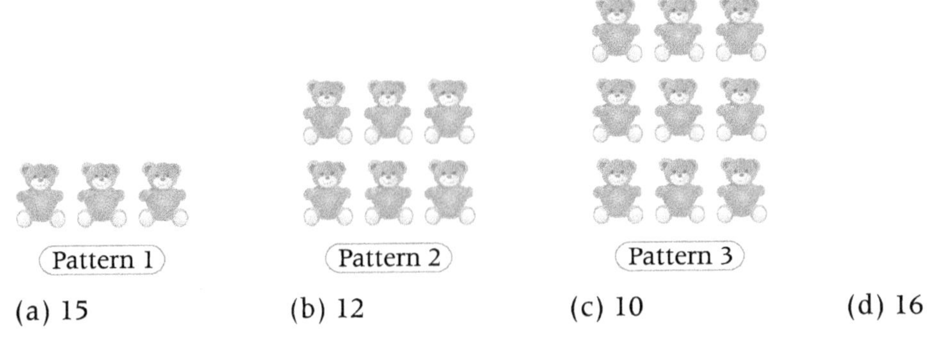

Pattern 1　　　Pattern 2　　　Pattern 3

(a) 15　　　　(b) 12　　　　(c) 10　　　　(d) 16

5. Which glass of water should come next in the pattern shown below?

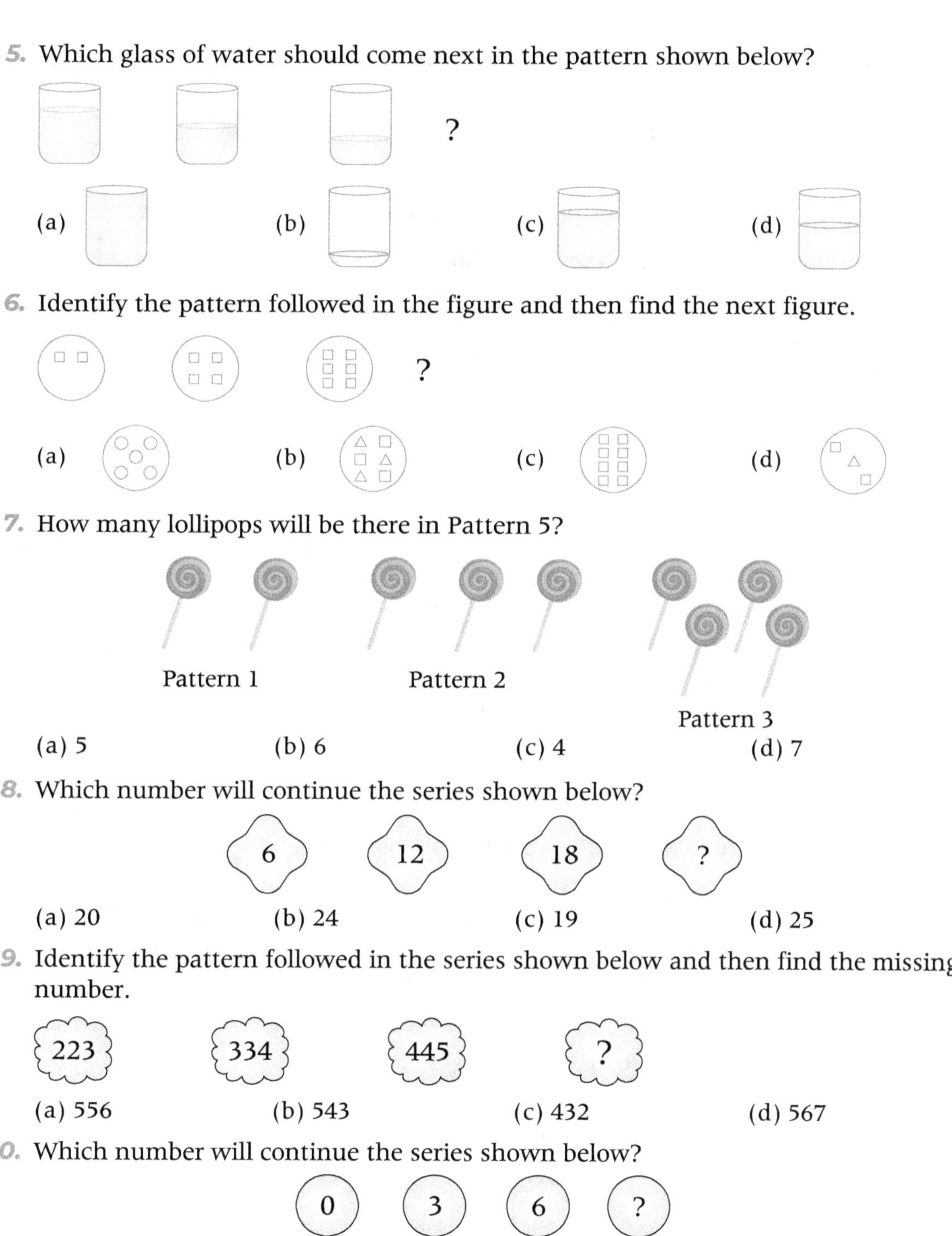

(a)   (b)   (c)   (d)

6. Identify the pattern followed in the figure and then find the next figure.

(a)   (b)   (c)   (d)

7. How many lollipops will be there in Pattern 5?

Pattern 1   Pattern 2

Pattern 3

(a) 5   (b) 6   (c) 4   (d) 7

8. Which number will continue the series shown below?

6   12   18   ?

(a) 20   (b) 24   (c) 19   (d) 25

9. Identify the pattern followed in the series shown below and then find the missing number.

223   334   445   ?

(a) 556   (b) 543   (c) 432   (d) 567

10. Which number will continue the series shown below?

0   3   6   ?

(a) 8   (b) 9   (c) 10   (d) 11

11. Which number will continue the series shown below?

23   18   13   ?

(a) 11   (b) 8
(c) 9   (d) 6

12. Which number will continue the series shown below?

2   4   8   ?

(a) 12   (b) 10
(c) 14   (d) 16

13. Which number will continue the series shown below?

16   8   4   ?

(a) 6   (b) 5
(c) 4   (d) 2

14. Which number will replace the question mark in the number pattern given below?

100   81   64   49   ?

(a) 16   (b) 36
(c) 64   (d) 4

15. Find the missing number in the given number pattern?

9   18   36   72   ?

(a) 244   (b) 286
(c) 144   (d) 388

16. Which letter will come in the last paper held by the girl?

K   M   O   ?

(a) Q   (b) L
(c) P   (d) N

17. Some letters are written in the pictures shown below following a pattern and form a series. Which letters from the given alternatives will continue the series?

MD   NE   OF   ?

(a) JP   (b) TH
(c) QP   (d) PG

18. A letter's series is shown below. Find the pair of letters that will continue the series.

PQ   RS   TU   ?

(a) VW   (b) XY   (c) WX   (d) WY

Directions (Q. Nos. 19-22) Find the next pair of letters in the series.

19. GB   HC   ID   JE   ?

(a) IJ   (b) KF   (c) FK   (d) GH

20. QL   NN   KP   ?

(a) HR   (b) RH   (c) JP   (d) PJ

21. Some letters are shown below which follow a certain pattern. Based on that find that group which will continue the series.

TAF   TEF   TIF   TOF   ?

(a) POT   (b) TUF   (c) AUT   (d) BTF

22. A group of letters shown below, which follow a certain pattern. Based on that find those letters which will continue the series.

JASU   KBTV   LCUW   ?

(a) TORF   (b) NOQZ   (c) DEPQ   (d) STOP

Coding-Decoding

Coding is a method of conveying a message in secret way. Decoding is a process of break the code to understand the conveyed message.

In this chapter, figures and letters are coded following a certain rule. In the same manner it is required to find the code for the figure or letters asked in the question.

EXAMPLE 1 Observe the figures and their codes given below and then answer the question based on it.

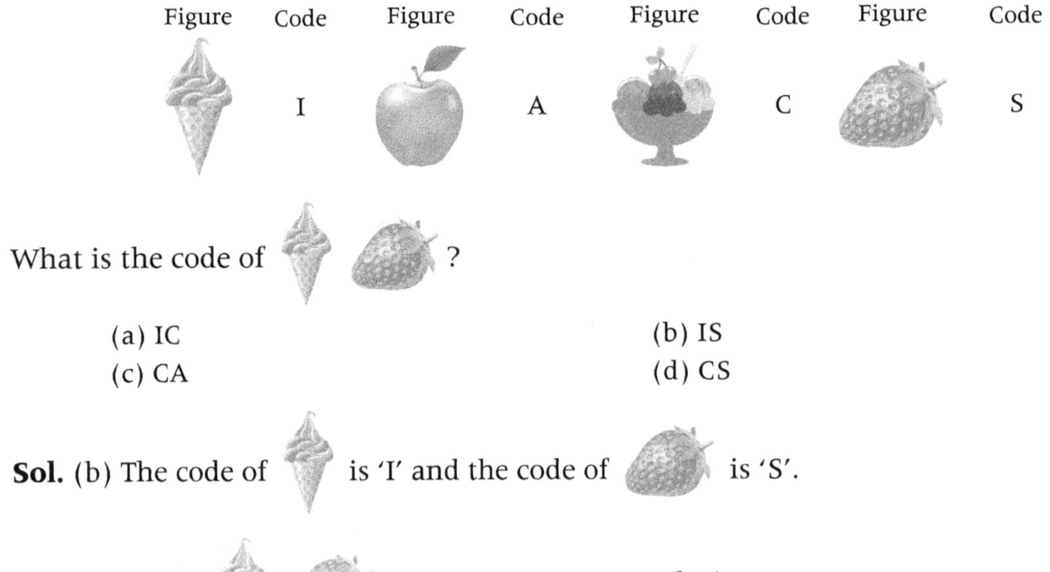

What is the code of ?

(a) IC
(b) IS
(c) CA
(d) CS

Sol. (b) The code of is 'I' and the code of is 'S'.

So, the code of is 'IS'. Hence, option (b) is correct.

EXAMPLE 2 If 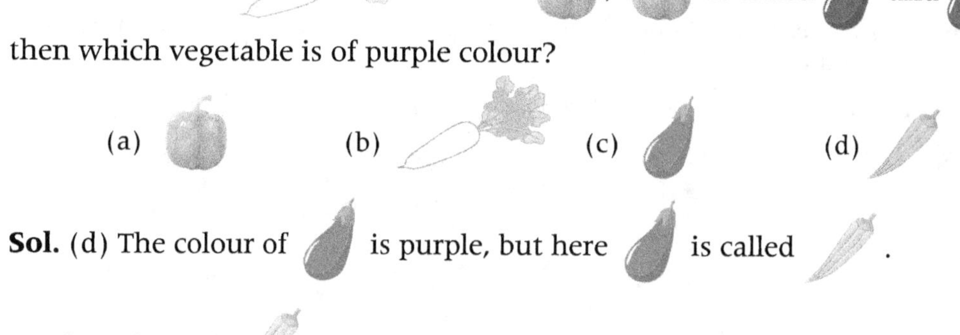 is called , is called and is called ,

then which vegetable is of purple colour?

   (a)   (b)   (c)   (d)

Sol. (d) The colour of is purple, but here is called .

So, the colour of is purple. Hence, option (d) is correct.

EXAMPLE 3 Some letters and their codes are given in the table below.

Letters	A	B	C	D	E	F	G	M	N	O
Codes	6	p	s	i	@	m	v	e	8	x

What is the code of 'MANGO'?

(a) ex6v8   (b) @psim   (c) e68vx   (d) @6v8m

Sol. (c) From the given table,

$$M \rightarrow e, \ A \rightarrow 6, \ N \rightarrow 8, \ G \rightarrow v, \ O \rightarrow x$$

So, the code of 'MANGO' is 'e68vx'. Hence, option (c) is correct.

EXAMPLE 4 If 'Monday' is called 'Sunday' and 'Sunday' is called 'Tuesday', then on which day we celebrate international holiday?

(a) Monday   (b) Sunday

(c) Wednesday   (d) Tuesday

Sol. (d) We celebrate international holiday on 'Sunday' but here 'Sunday' is called 'Tuesday'. So, we celebrate international holiday on 'Tuesday'.

Hence, option (d) is correct.

⏰ Let's Practice

Directions (Q. Nos. 1-3) Some figures and their codes are shown below. Based on these answer the questions that follow.

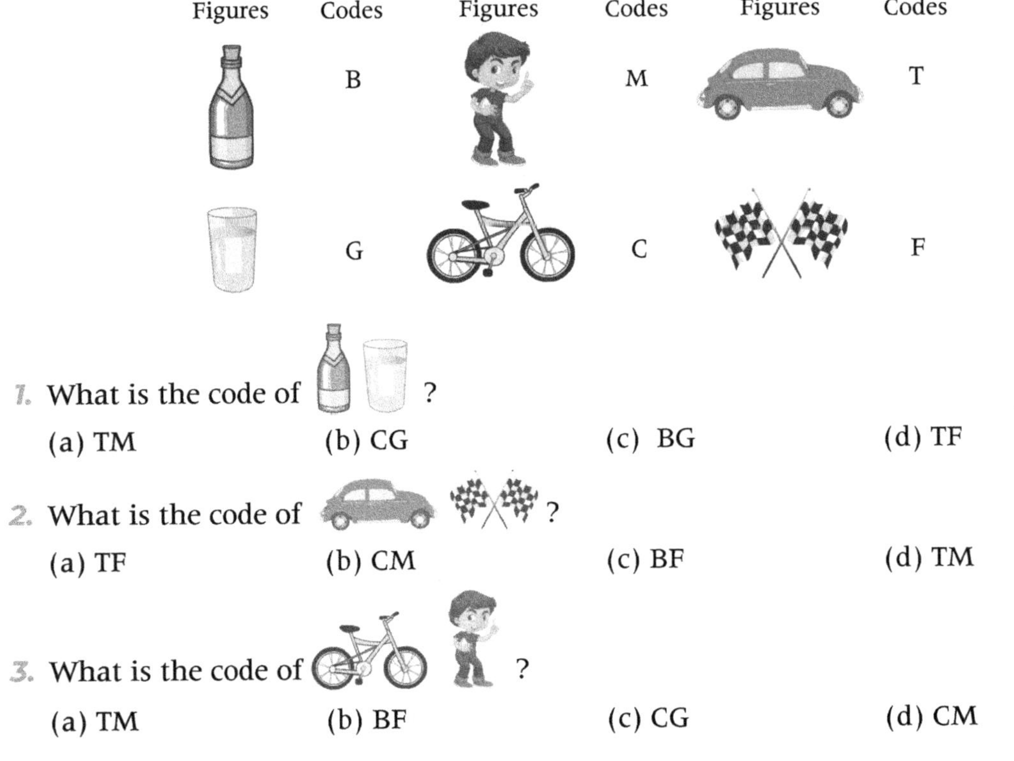

Figures	Codes	Figures	Codes	Figures	Codes
(bottle)	B	(boy)	M	(car)	T
(glass)	G	(bicycle)	C	(flags)	F

1. What is the code of (bottle)(glass) ?
   (a) TM   (b) CG   (c) BG   (d) TF

2. What is the code of (car)(flags) ?
   (a) TF   (b) CM   (c) BF   (d) TM

3. What is the code of (bicycle)(boy) ?
   (a) TM   (b) BF   (c) CG   (d) CM

Directions (Q. Nos. 4-6) Capital letters from A to Z with their codes are given in the table shown below. Based on the table answer the questions that follow.

Letters	A	B	C	D	E	F	G	H	I	J	K	L	M
Codes	2	@	0	x	4	i	✡	9	a	b	+	6	g
Letters	N	O	P	Q	R	S	T	U	V	W	X	Y	Z
Codes	1	©	e	3	#	h	$	8	7	f	–	d	5

4. What is the code of PARENT?
   (a) $f - b + 63$ (b) $e2\#41\$$
   (c) $h\$x49g$ (d) $c\#e12b$

5. What is the code of COUNT?
   (a) $+6a1©$ (b) $@810\$$
   (c) $©@3\#1$ (d) $0©81\$$

6. In a certain code the following number are coded by assigning signs.

Numbers	5	4	3	2	1
Signs	+	÷	×	−	=

What is the code for the number 3425?

(a) × ÷ + −   (b) × ÷ − +   (c) = ÷ + −   (d) ÷ × − =

7. If 'Yellow' is called 'Black' and 'Black' is called 'Green', then what is the colour of sky at night?

(a) Green   (b) Yellow   (c) Red   (d) Orange

8. If 'Fan' is 'chair' and 'chair' is 'roof', on which of the following will a person sit?

(a) Roof   (b) Chair   (c) Fan   (d) Pen

9. If bat is racket and racket is football, what is cricket played with?

(a) Bat   (b) Racket   (c) Football   (d) Shuttle

10. If △ means ◯ and ◯ means ▢ , then which of the following geometrical shapes is ring?

(a) ▢   (b) △   (c) ▢   (d) ⬠

11. If 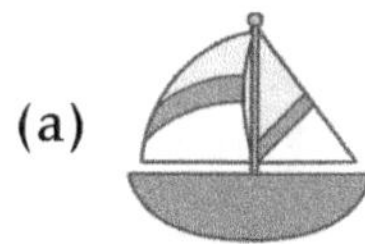 is called  and  is called  , then which vehicle is two wheeler?

(a)   (b)   (c)   (d)

12. If 'CHEER' means 'REEHC' and 'MONKEY' means 'YEKNOM', then what is the code for 'CHAIR'?

(a) RIAHC   (b) RIACH   (c) RAICH   (d) RICHA

13. If 'APPLE' is coded as 'BQQMF', then what is the code for 'MANGO'?

(a) NBOHP   (b) BNOPH   (c) HPOBN   (d) HPNBO

14. If MOON is coded as 4 and BRAIN is coded as 5, then what is the code for ABHISHEK?

(a) 4   (b) 6   (c) 7   (d) 8

15. If 'RAMAN' is written as '45652' and 'CHAMAN' is written as '315652', then what is the code for 'MAN'?

(a) 625   (b) 265   (c) 562   (d) 652

Chapter 05

Alphabet and Word Formation Test

In this chapter, questions are asked from alphabet, i.e. English letters and words. This chapter, deals with the following questions :

- To form meaningful words on filling the following blank space.
- Finding the word, which can or cannot be formed from the letters of the given word.
- Arranging the letters to form meaningful word and also finding their category to which the meaningful word belongs.
- Questions related to letter series.

EXAMPLE 1 A block consisting of two letters are shown below. A block is added after the block having a letter that makes only one meaningful word which is an animal. Find that letter.

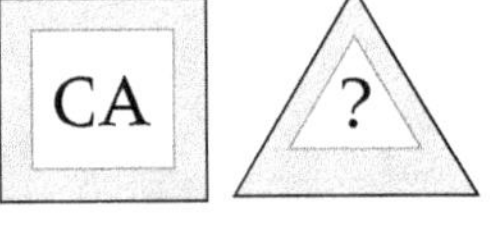

(a) M (b) R (c) D (d) T

Sol. (d) Block after first block must carry the letter 'T' that makes meaningful word CAT. Which is an animal. Hence, option (d) is correct.

EXAMPLE 2 A banner hanging outside the computer shop is shown below :

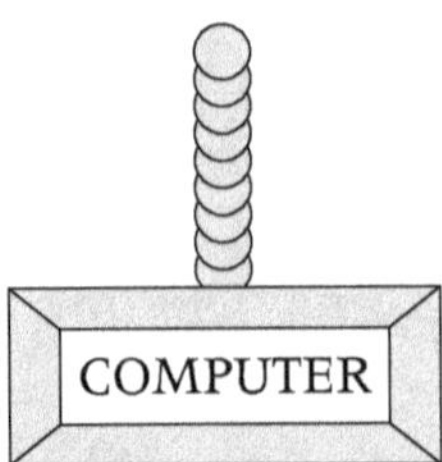

Identify the word from the given alternatives that can be formed using the letters of the word 'COMPUTER'.

    (a) TIRE   (b) RATE   (c) MUTE   (d) CART

Sol. (c) 'MUTE' word can be formed using the letters of the word 'COMPUTER'. Hence, option (c) is correct.

EXAMPLE 3 In the following options find the word that cannot be made from the letters of the given word.

TEACHER

    (a) CHAIR   (b) HEAR   (c) REACH   (d) EACH

Sol. (a) 'CHAIR' word cannot be formed using the letters of the word 'TEACHER' because 'I' is not present in the given word.

EXAMPLE 4 Figures shown below consists of letters and numbers below them. Arrange them in a way that they form a meaningful word and find the combination of numbers of the word so formed.

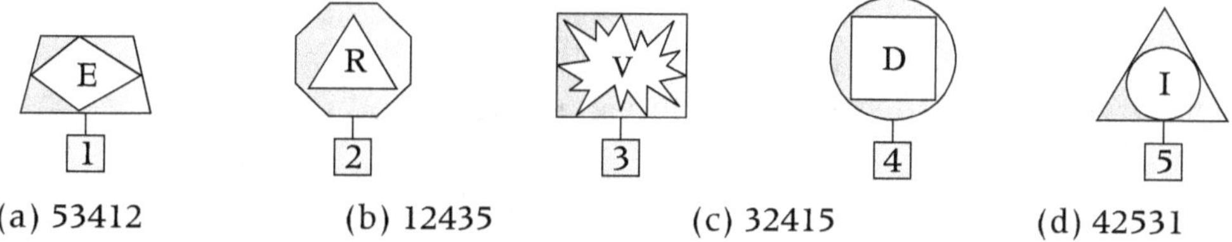

    (a) 53412   (b) 12435   (c) 32415   (d) 42531

Sol. (d) Considering option (d),

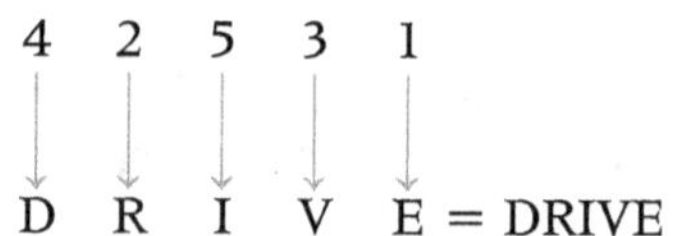

So, after arranging the numbers, '42531' we get a meaningful word 'DRIVE'. Hence, option (d) is correct.

EXAMPLE 5 Four letters are shown below :

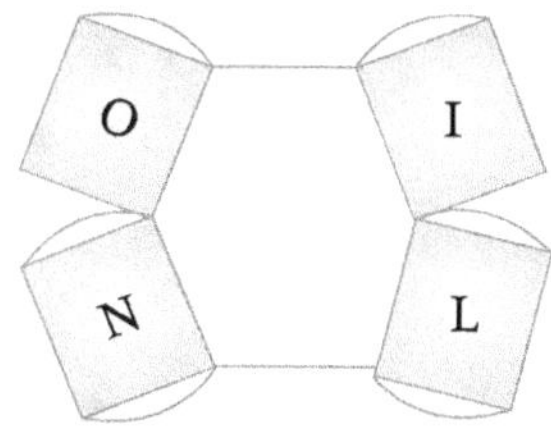

Arrange them in a way that they form a meaningful word and then find its category.

    (a) Animal   (b) Fruit   (c) Flower   (d) Vegetable

Sol. (a) The letters when arranged will form a word 'LION', which is an animal. Hence, option (a) is correct.

EXAMPLE 6. In which of the following series, the number of letters skipped between adjacent letters is same.

    (a) DEGI   (b) ORSU   (c) ACFG   (d) SVYB

Sol. (d) Considering option (d),

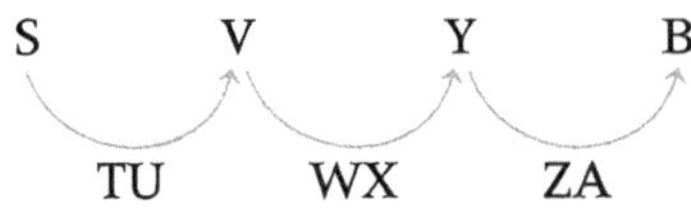

So, number of letters skipped between adjacent letters is same. Hence option (d) is correct.

⏰ Let's Practice

1. Find the letter, which will end the first word and start the second word.

O	N	?	A	T

    (a) M   (b) R   (c) E   (d) L

2. Which letter will end the first word and start the second word?

M A L ? A K E

    (a) C   (b) E   (c) F   (d) L

3. Which letter from the given alternatives when replaced with question mark (?) will form one name of vegetable and one name of fruit?

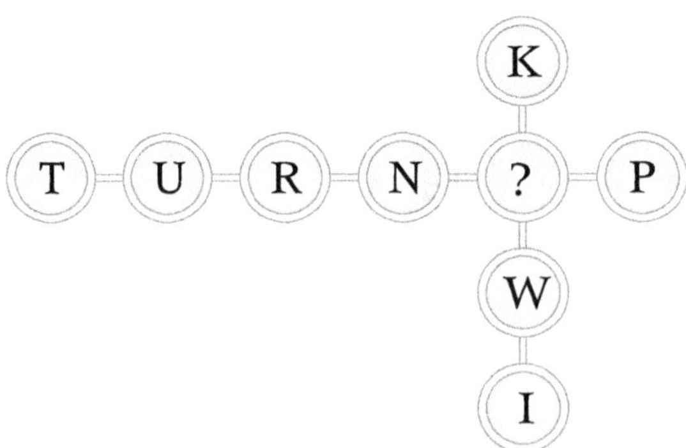

    (a) A   (b) I   (c) L   (d) E

4. Find the letter, which should be replaced with question mark (?) to make the name of two amphibians.

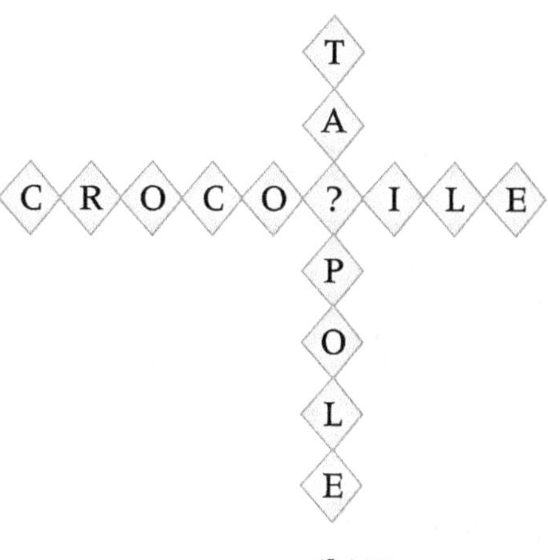

(a) K   (b) T
(c) M   (d) D

5. Choose the category of the word so formed after arranging the given letters.

(a) Fruit   (b) Flower
(c) Cloth   (d) Month

6. Identify the category of the word so formed after arranging the given letters.

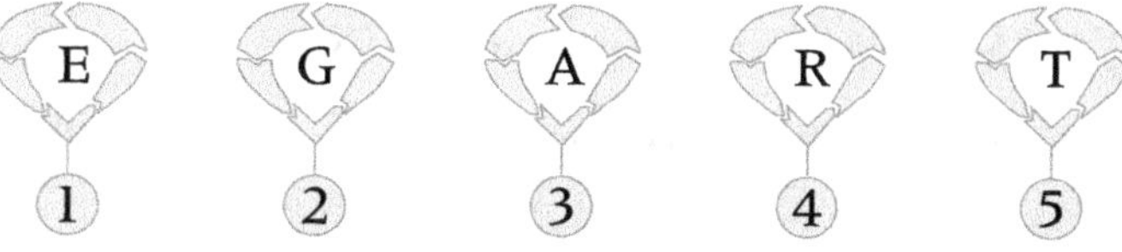

(a) Flower   (b) Month
(c) Sport   (d) Cloth

7. Choose the correct combination of numbers, so that letters when arranged form a meaningful word. **Hint** That word starts with letter 'G'.

E   G   A   R   T
1   2   3   4   5

(a) 43125   (b) 24135
(c) 31254   (d) 42153

8. A child holds the following balloons in its hand. Some letters and numbers are written on the balloons. How the letters should be arranged, so that they form a meaningful word? Find the combination of numbers.

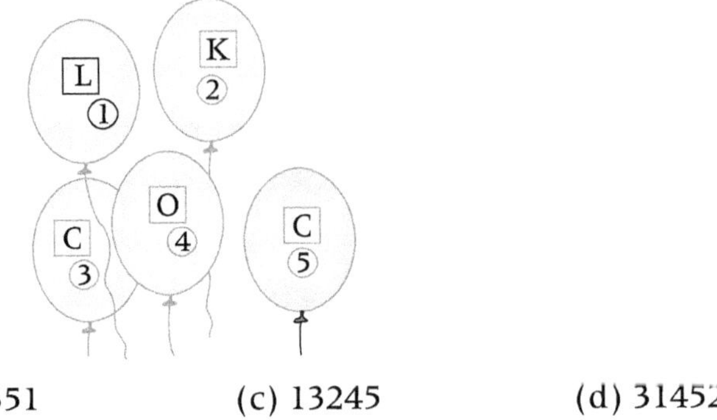

(a) 43215　　　　(b) 24351　　　　(c) 13245　　　　(d) 31452

Directions (Q. Nos. 9 and 10) Choose the correct combination of numbers. So, that letters when arranged form a meaningful word.

9.

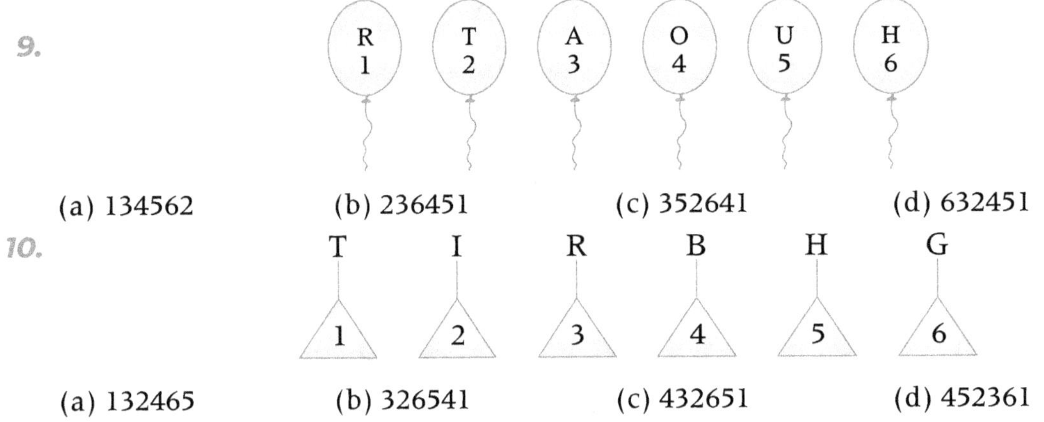

(a) 134562　　　　(b) 236451　　　　(c) 352641　　　　(d) 632451

10.

(a) 132465　　　　(b) 326541　　　　(c) 432651　　　　(d) 452361

11. Choose the word from the given alternatives, which can be formed using the letters of the given word.

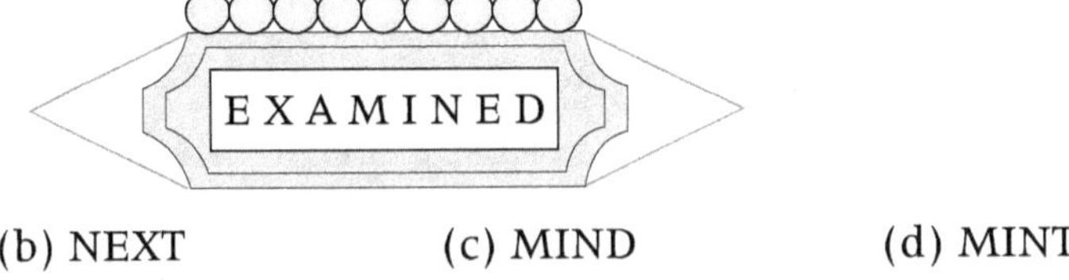

(a) EXTRA　　　　(b) NEXT　　　　(c) MIND　　　　(d) MINT

12. Find the word from the given alternatives, which can be formed using the letters of the given word.

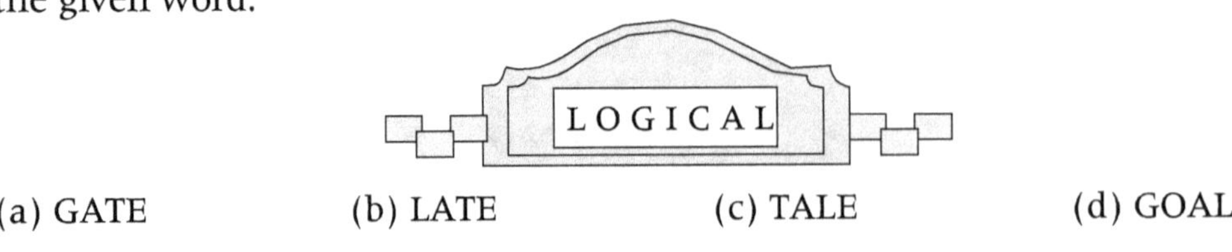

(a) GATE　　　　(b) LATE　　　　(c) TALE　　　　(d) GOAL

Directions (Q. Nos. 13 and 14) Find the word from the given alternatives, which can be formed using the letters of the given word.

13.

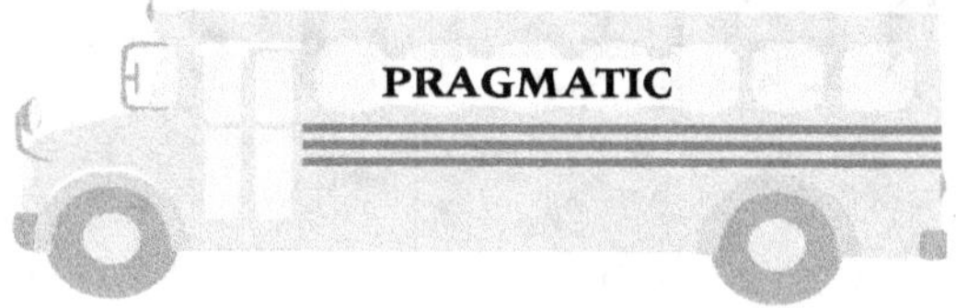

(a) ANIMAL (b) EXAMINER (c) NATIONAL (d) ANIMATION

14.

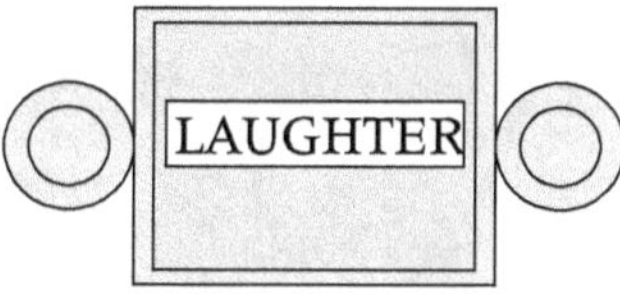

(a) GUITAR (b) AGMARK
(c) GAME (d) MAGIC

15. Identify the word, which cannot be formed using the letters of the given word.

(a) HEAL (b) REAL
(c) GAME (d) LATER

16. Which word from the given alternatives cannot be formed using the letters of the given word?

(a) RACE (b) EASY (c) NICE (d) ESSAY

Directions (Q. Nos. 17 and 18) In which of the following series, the number of letters skipped between adjacent letters is same?

17. (a) IJKL (b) LMPT (c) SVWB (d) IKLP

18. (a) DEHL (b) OQSU (c) ZAYZ (d) CDAF

Complete the Figure

Complete the figure by drawing its incomplete part by following some rules.

EXAMPLE 1 Choose the figure from the given alternatives that will complete the given figure.

(a)   (b)   (c)   (d)

Sol. (b) The given pattern can be completed by using the figure in option (b).

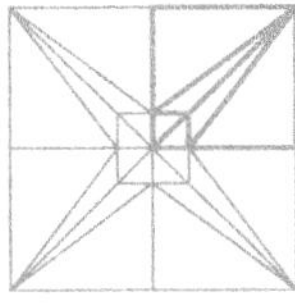

EXAMPLE 2 Which of the following options will complete the figure(X)?

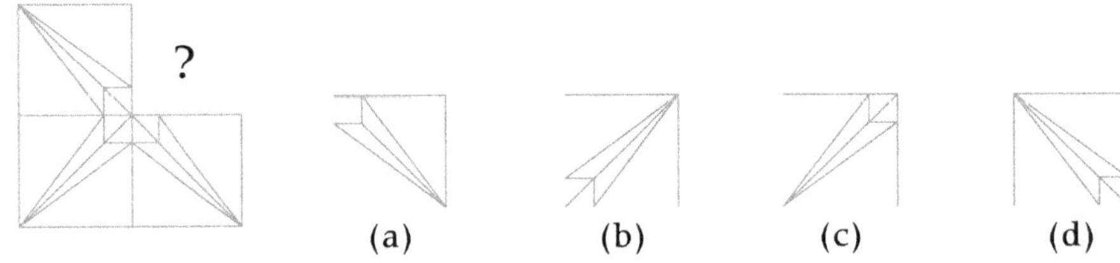

(a)   (b)   (c)   (d)

(X)

Sol. (c) The figure (X) will complete by using the option (c) figure.

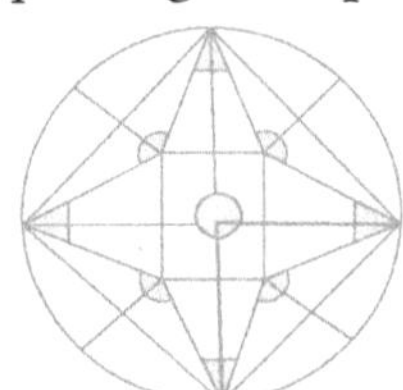

⏰ Let's Practice

1. Identify the figure from the options that will complete the given pattern.

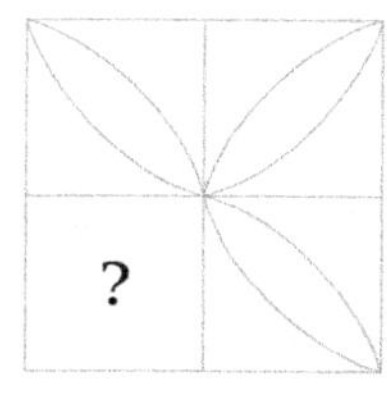 ?   (a) 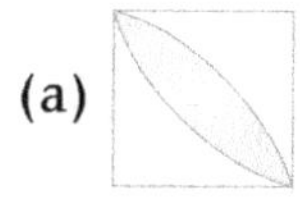   (b) 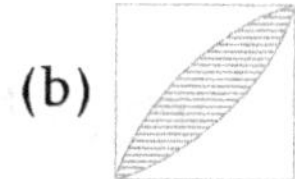   (c)    (d) 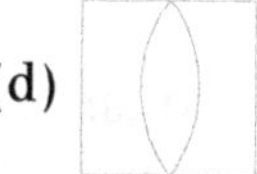

2. Choose the figure from the given alternatives that will complete the given pattern.

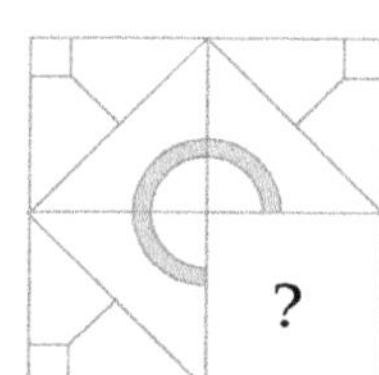 ?   (a) 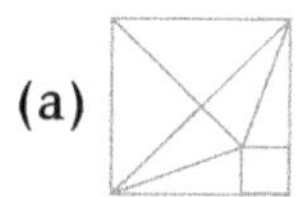   (b) 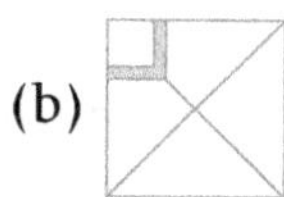   (c) 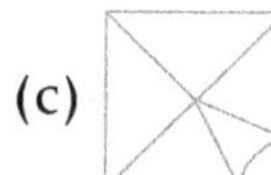   (d) 

3. Identify the figure from the options that will complete the given pattern.

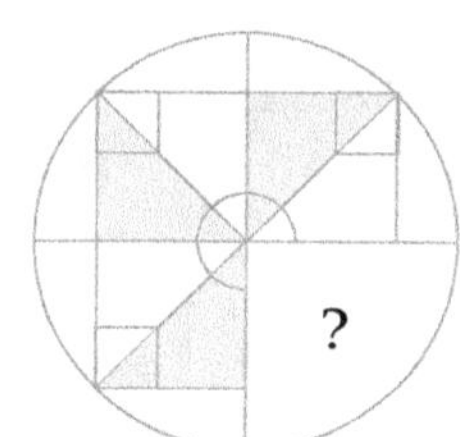 ?   (a) 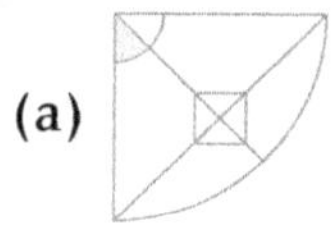   (b) 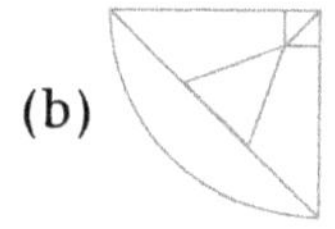   (c) 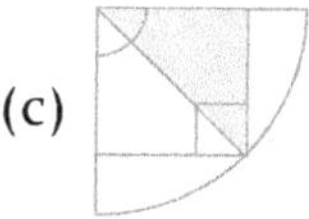   (d) 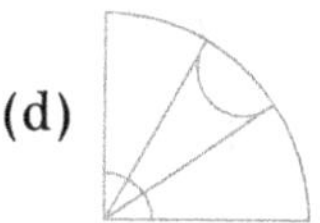

4. Which of the following option will complete the given pattern?

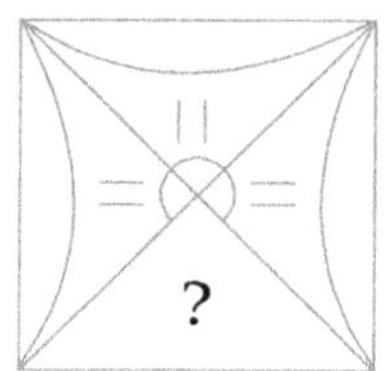 ?   (a) 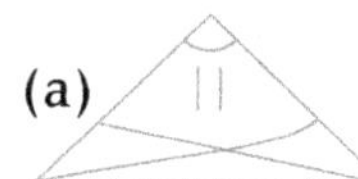   (b)    (c) 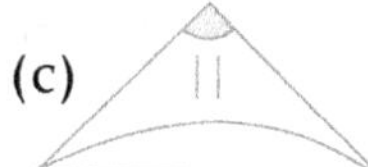   (d) 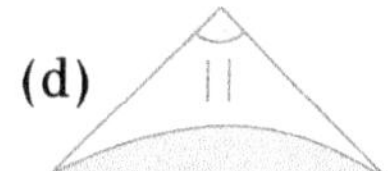

5. Which of the following options will complete the given pattern?

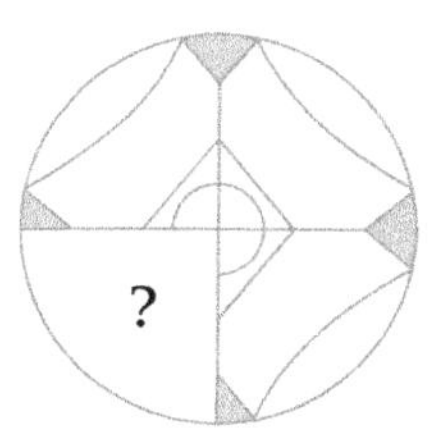 ?   (a) 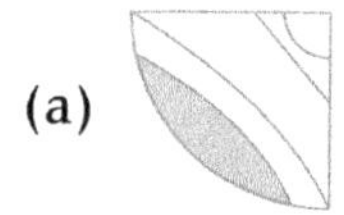   (b) 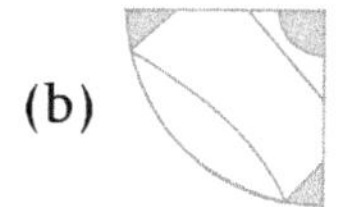   (c) 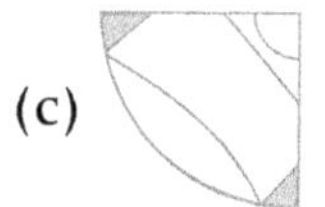   (d) 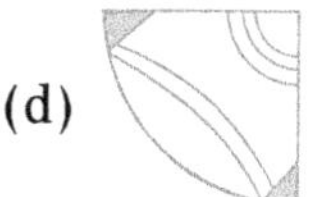

6. Which of the following options will complete the given pattern?

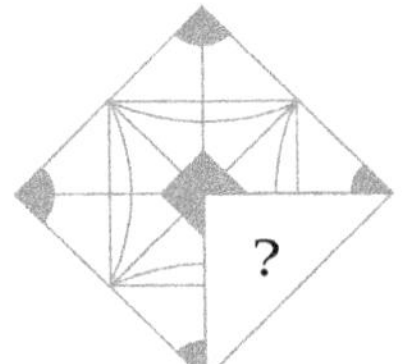   (a) 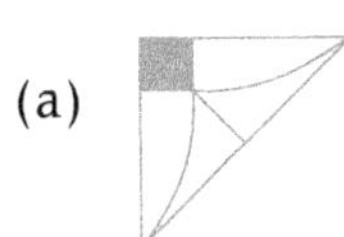   (b) 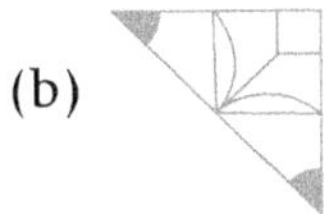   (c) 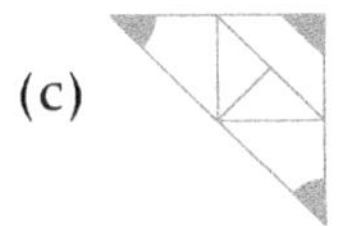   (d) 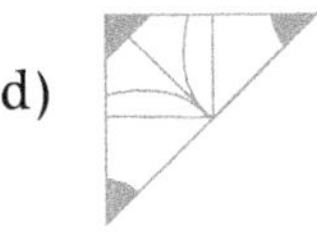

7. A cloth consists of the following pattern from which a part is missing. Find that missing part of the pattern.

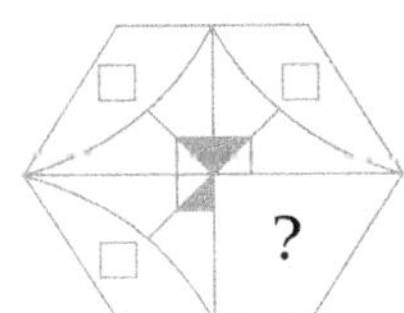   (a)    (b) 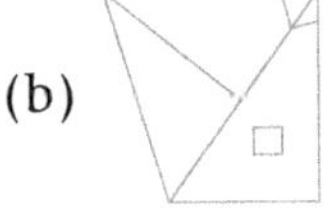   (c) 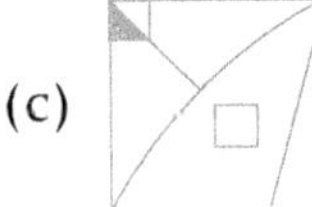   (d) 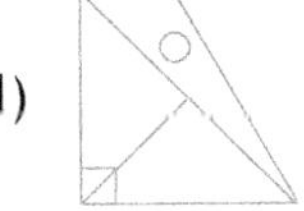

8. Which of the following options will complete the given pattern?

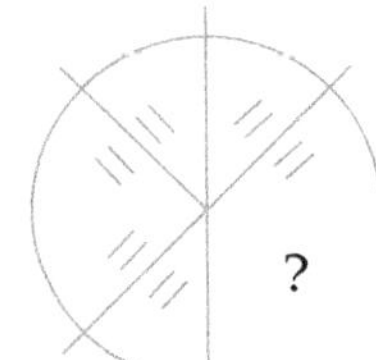   (a) 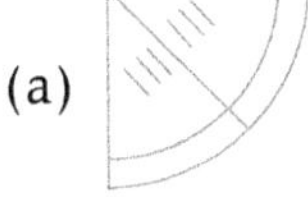   (b) 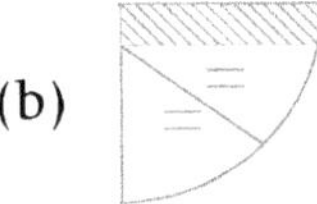   (c) 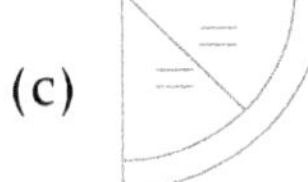   (d) 

9. Identify the figure from the options that will complete the given pattern?

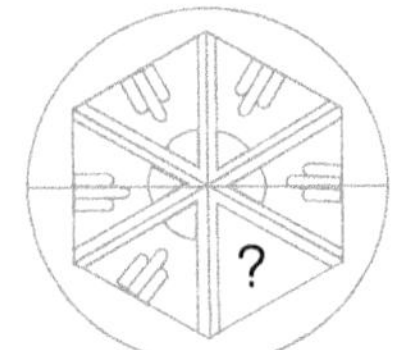   (a) 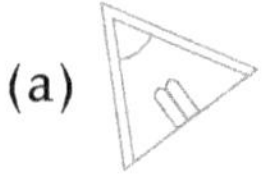   (b) 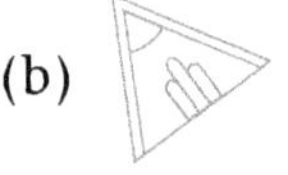   (c) 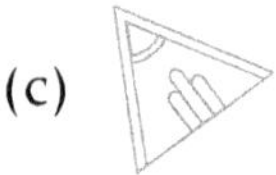   (d) 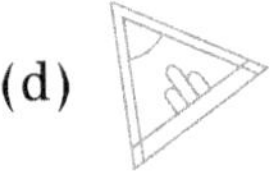

10. Which of the following options will complete the given pattern?

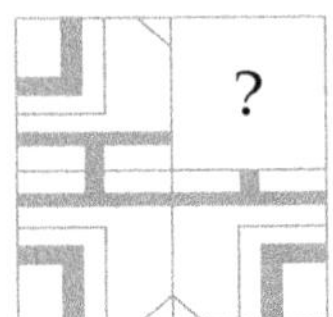   (a) 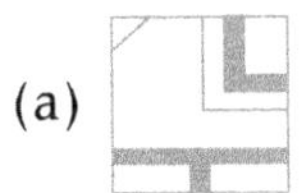   (b) 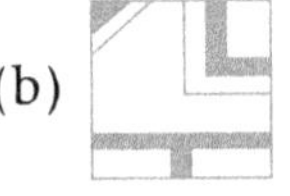   (c) 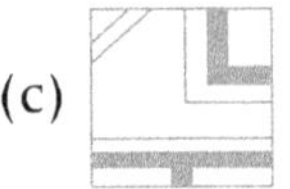   (d) 

Hidden Figures

Hidden Figures includes two types of questions. First is, finding the question part in the option figures and second is, finding which part from the options is hidden in the question figure.

EXAMPLE 1 Lina draw a figure on a piece of paper and find that figure exists in any of the given pictures shown below. Find the picture in which the given part is hidden.

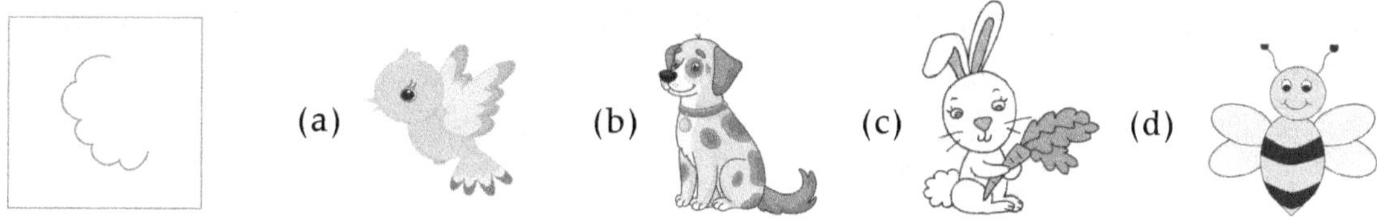

(a)   (b)   (c)   (d)

Sol. (c) The given part is hidden in option (c) as shown in **adjacent figure**. Hence, option (c) is correct.

EXAMPLE 2 A pattern is made on a fibre sheet as shown below. Find a figure from the options which is exactly hidden in the given pattern.

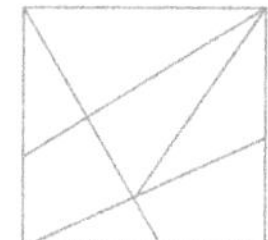

(a) 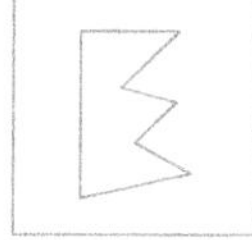 (b)  (c) 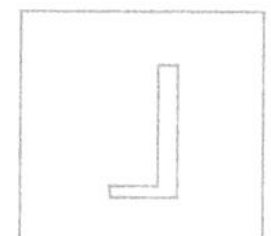 (d) 

Sol. (b) Figure in option (b) is exactly hidden in the given pattern as shown in adjacent figure. Hence, option (b) is correct.

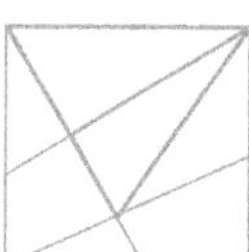

Let's Practice

1. In which of the following pictures the given shape (X) is hidden?

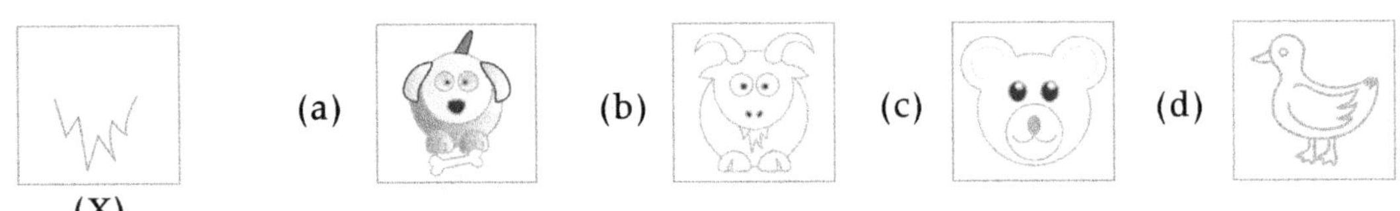

(X)   (a)   (b)   (c)   (d)

2. Look at the shape shown below and find the picture from the options in which it is hidden.

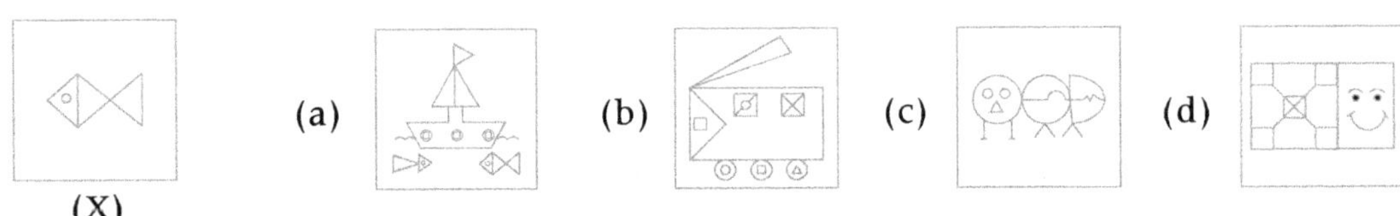

(X)   (a)   (b)   (c)   (d)

3. Dany finds a same part of a toy as shown below. Find the toy to which this part belongs.

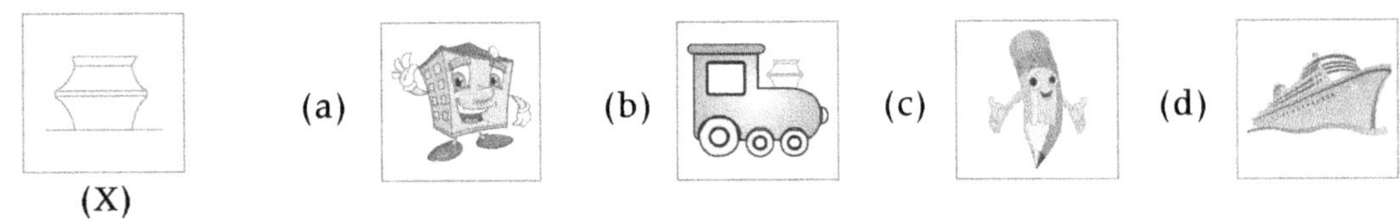

(X)   (a)   (b)   (c)   (d)

4. Identify the figure from the given options in which the given shape (X) is hidden.

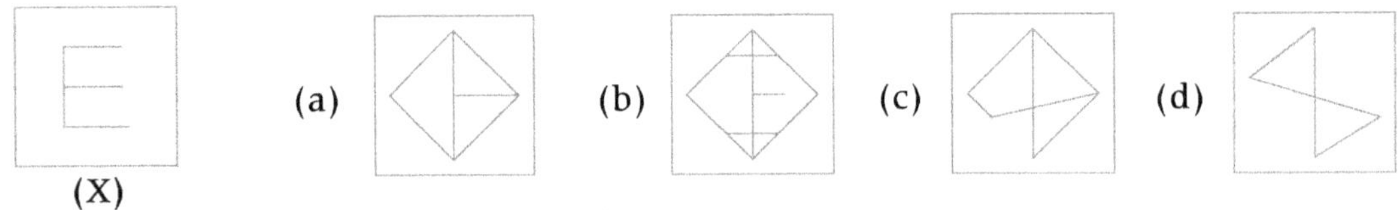

(X)   (a)   (b)   (c)   (d)

5. Find the figure from the given options in which the given shape (X) is hidden.

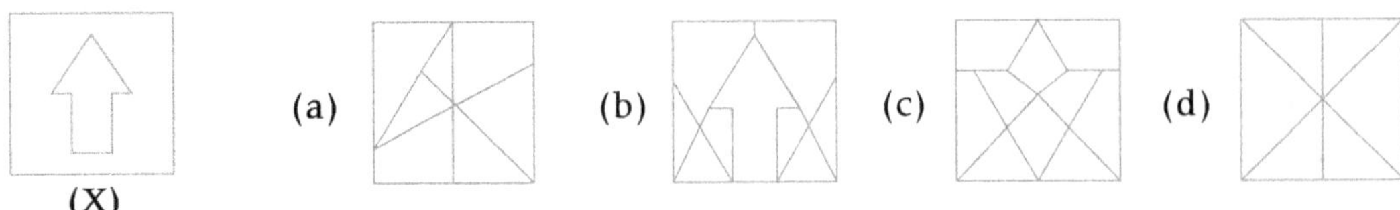

(X)   (a)   (b)   (c)   (d)

6. In which of the following figures, the given shape (X) is hidden as one of its part?

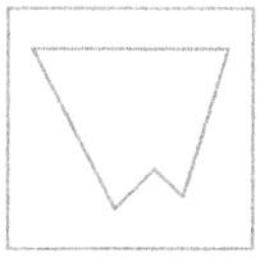

(X)

(a)    (b) 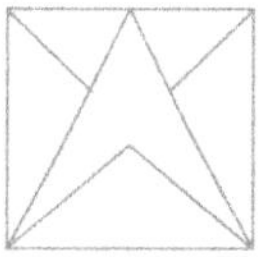   (c) 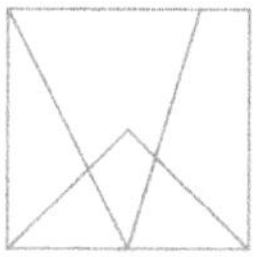   (d)

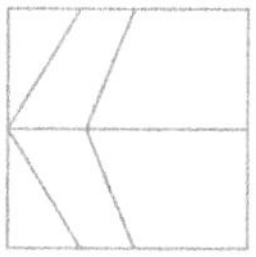

7. Luca draw a shape on a sheet of paper. Find in which of the following figures the given shape (X) is hidden.

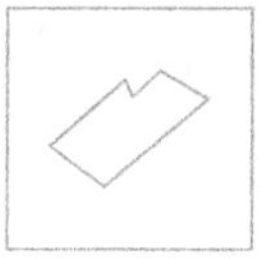

(X)

(a) 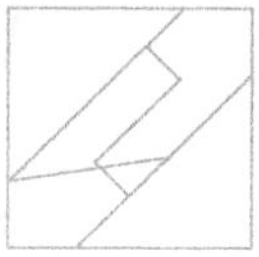   (b) 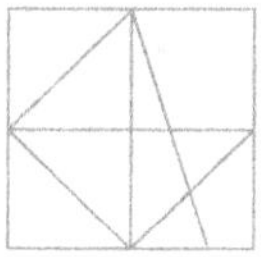   (c) 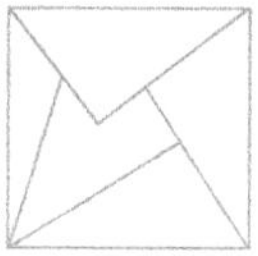   (d)

8. A part of the main figure is shown below. Find the figure from the options to which it belongs.

(X)

(a) 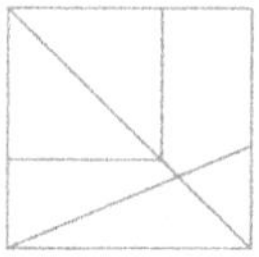   (b) 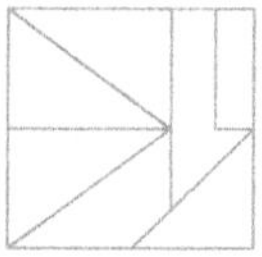   (c) 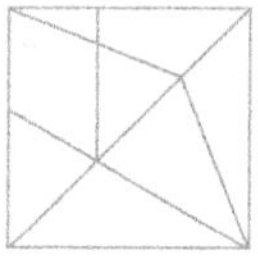   (d)

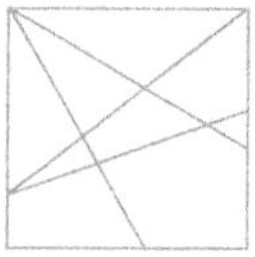

9. Following figure is given below in a triangle shaped pattern. Find from the options, which figure is hidden in the triangle shaped pattern.

(X)

(a) 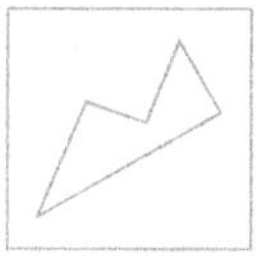   (b) 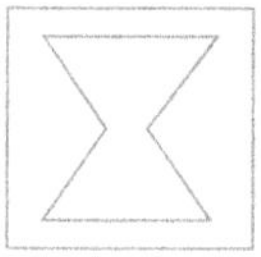   (c)    (d)

10. Identify the figure from the options which is hidden in figure (X).

(X)

(a) 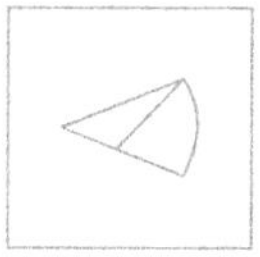   (b) 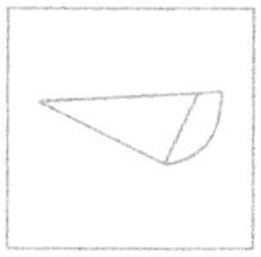   (c) 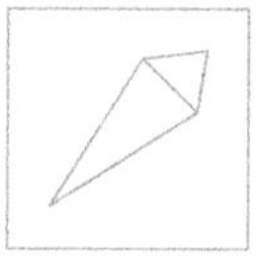   (d)

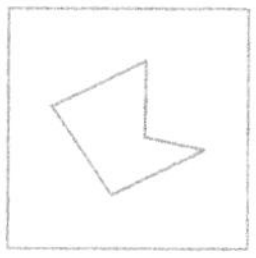

11. Which figure from the given options is hidden in the figure (X)?

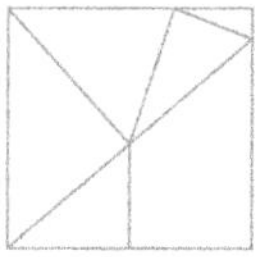

(X)

(a) 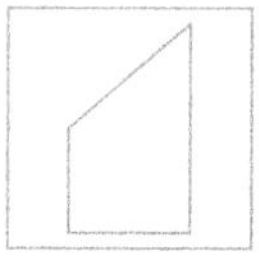   (b) 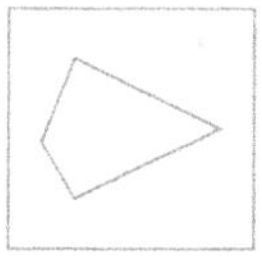   (c) 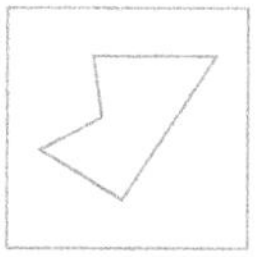   (d)

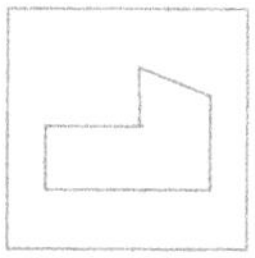

12. A book's front cover consists of the following figures as shown below. Find a figure from the given options, which is hidden in the figure shown below.

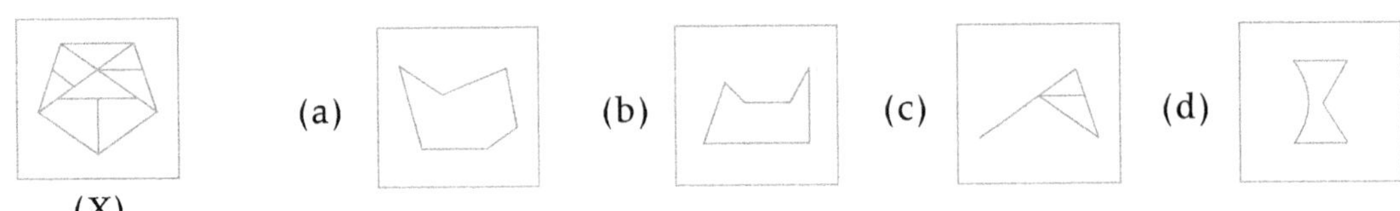

(X)

13. In which of the following options figure specified components of figure (X) are found?

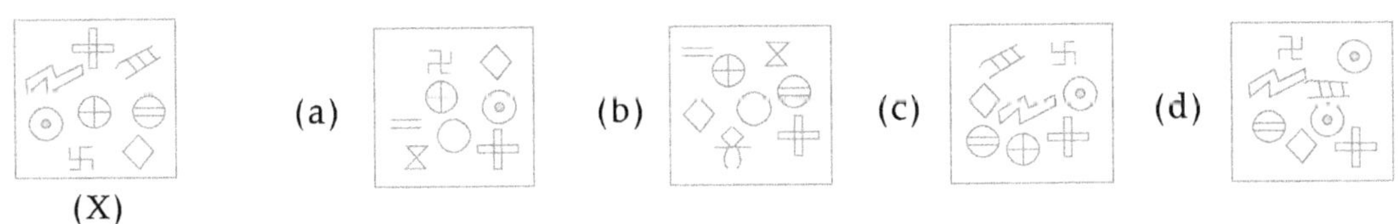

(X)

14. Identify the figure from the options is hidden in figure (X).

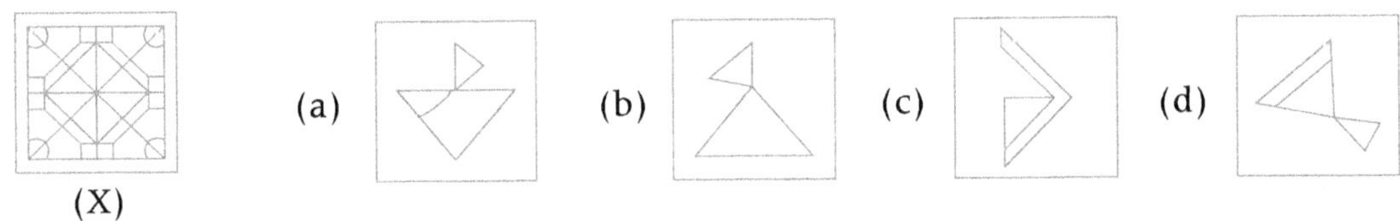

(X)

15. Which of the following alphabet is NOT embedded in the given figure (X)?

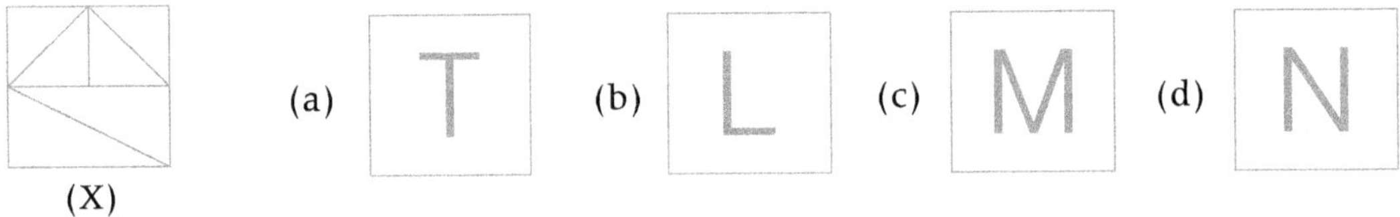

(X)

16. Which shape is NOT embedded in the given figure (X)?

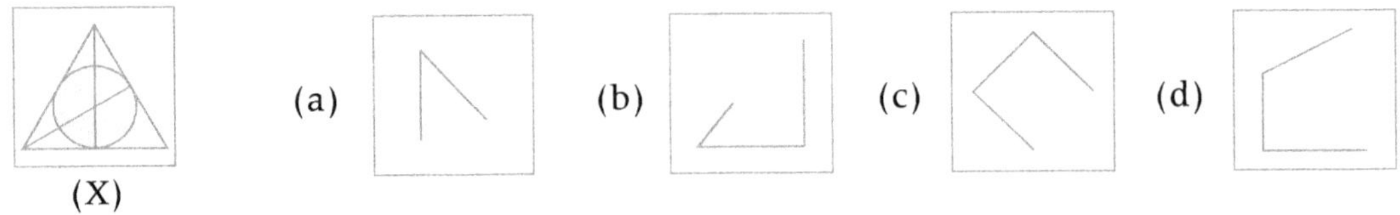

(X)

17. Which shape is NOT embedded in the given figure (X)?

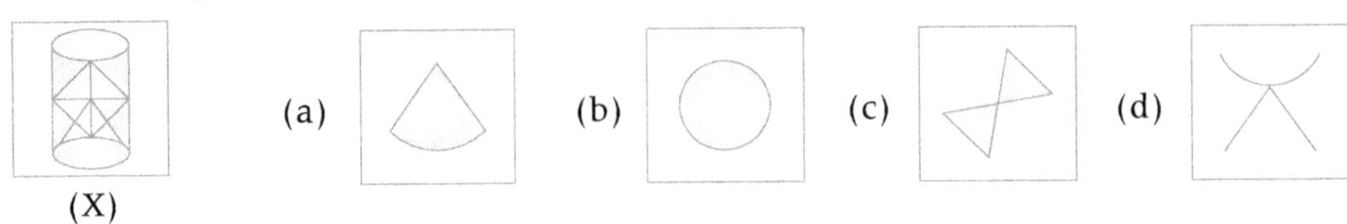

(X)

Counting of Figures

In this chapter, some figures are given and it is asked to count the number of lines, circles, triangles, squares, etc.

Let us observe some geometrical figures.

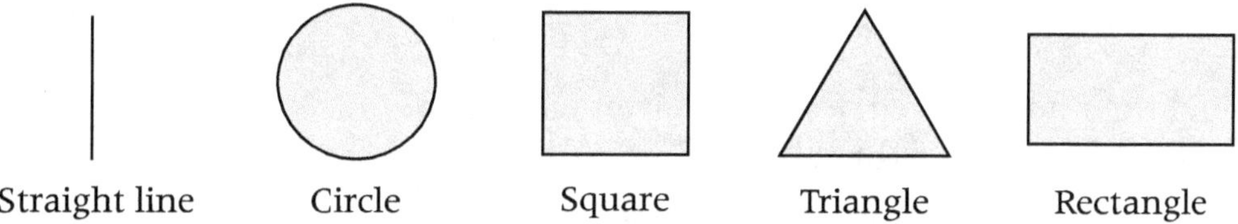

EXAMPLE 1 A figure shown below is drawn on a wall. Find the number of straight lines in the given figure.

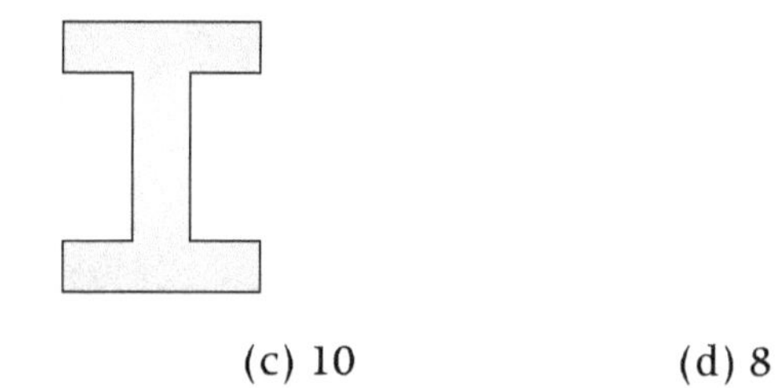

(a) 12   (b) 14   (c) 10   (d) 8

Sol. (a) The figure can be labelled as shown below :

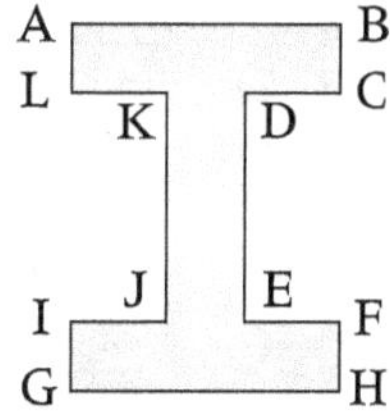

Number of straight lines = AB, BC, CD, DE, EF, FH, GH, GI, IJ, JK, KL and AL $= 12$

Hence, option (a) is correct.

Directions (Ex. Nos. 2 and 3) Look at the picture given below and answer the questions that follow.

2. Find the number of circles in the given picture.
   (a) 10   (b) 12   (c) 8   (d) 14

3. Count the number of rectangles in the given picture.
   (a) 8   (b) 10   (c) 13   (d) 11

Sol. (Ex. Nos. 2 and 3) The given picture can be labelled as shown below :

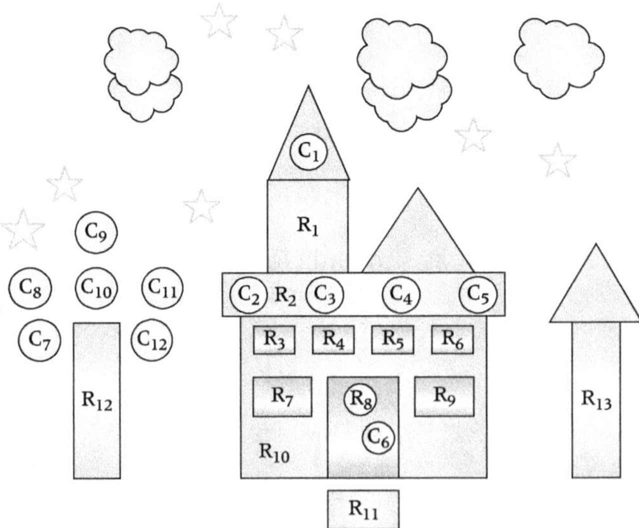

2. (b) Number of circles in the above picture is 12. Hence, option (b) is correct.

3. (c) Number of rectangles in the above picture is 13. Hence, option (c) is correct.

⏰ Let's Practice

1. A child is climbing the stairs as shown in the picture. Find the number of straight lines in it.
   - (a) 8
   - (b) 12
   - (c) 10
   - (d) 11

2. Count the different types of closed shapes in the given picture.
   - (a) 3
   - (b) 4
   - (c) 5
   - (d) 6

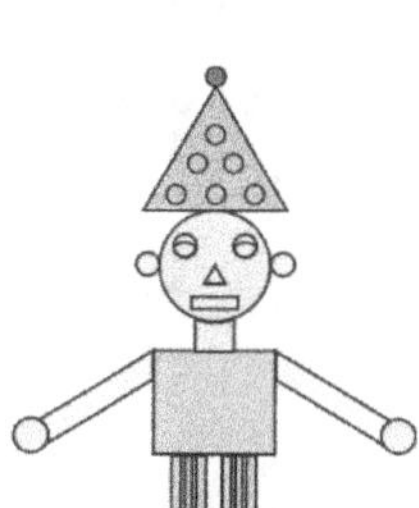

3. In the given picture, count the number of circles.
   - (a) 15
   - (b) 18
   - (c) 10
   - (d) 12

4. A picture is shown below. Find the number of circles in it.

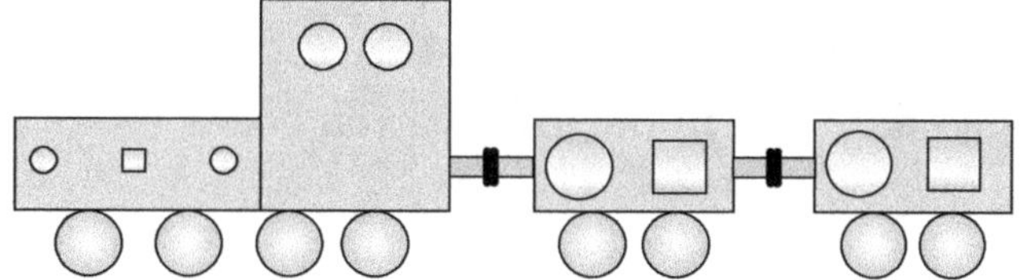

   - (a) 18
   - (c) 14
   - (b) 16
   - (d) 15

5. Find the number of rectangles in the given picture hanging on a wall.
   - (a) 6
   - (b) 7
   - (c) 8
   - (d) 5

6. A kite is kept on the floor. Find the number of triangles in it.
   (a) 22
   (b) 20
   (c) 18
   (d) 15

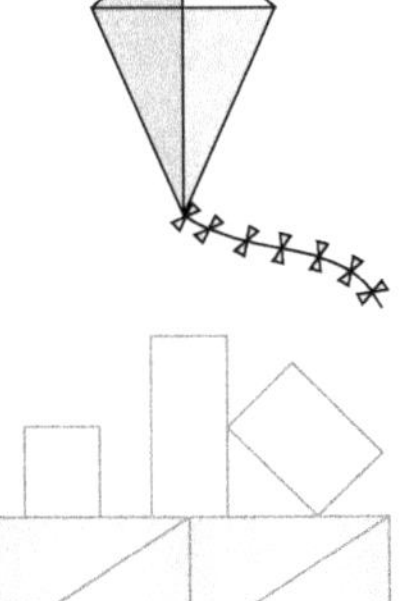

7. Count the number of rectangles and triangles in the picture shown below.
   (a) 6, 5
   (b) 5, 4
   (c) 6, 7
   (d) 7, 6

8. In the X-mas tree, how many slant lines are there?
   (a) 3
   (b) 4
   (c) 5
   (d) 6

9. Tany looks at the following picture and observes the different types of shapes. How many types of shapes are there in the picture?
   (a) 6
   (b) 3
   (c) 5
   (d) 4

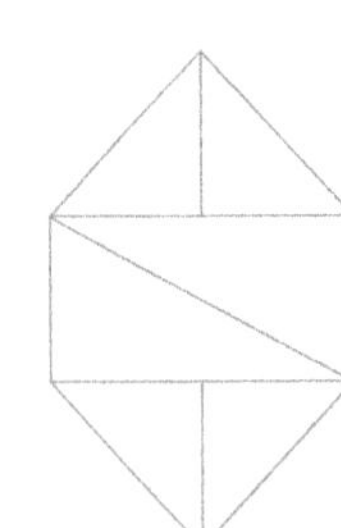

10. How many triangles are there in the image given below?
    (a) 8
    (b) 7
    (c) 6
    (d) 9

11. How many circles are there in the image given below?

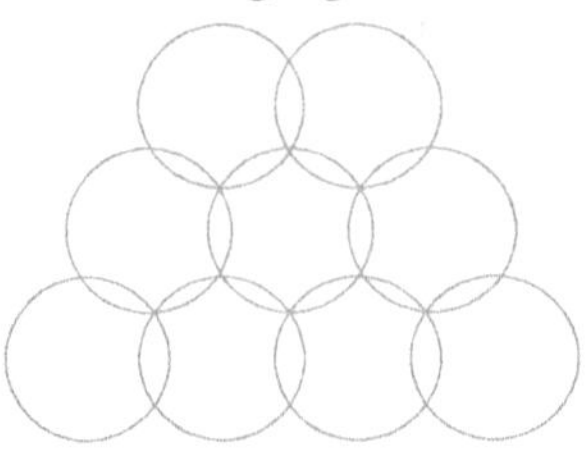

(a) 10   (b) 9   (c) 8   (d) 7

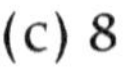

12. How many squares are there in image given below?

(a) 3   (b) 4   (c) 5   (d) 6

13. How many straight lines are there in image given below?

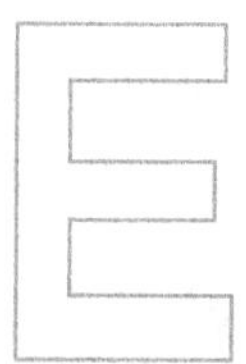

(a) 12   (b) 13   (c) 10   (d) 9

Directions (Q. Nos. 14 and 15) Look at the following picture and answer the questions given below.

14. Find the number of triangles in the given picture.
(a) 12   (b) 13   (c) 14   (d) 15

15. What is the difference between the number of triangles and number of circles in the given picture?
(a) 2   (b) 5   (c) 8   (d) 4

Grouping of Figures

Grouping of figures means having same type of figures in group. In this chapter you have to identify the figure from the given options which belongs to given 'group of figures'.

EXAMPLE 1 Select the figure below carefully and find the missing figure represented by question mark (?).

Sol. (b) Only option (b) has two lines inside the rectangle and both lines crosses each other. Hence, option (b) is correct.

EXAMPLE 2 Group the given figures into three classes using each figure only once.

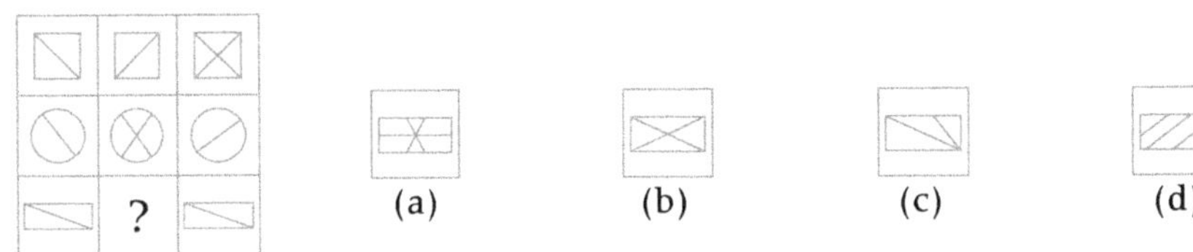

(a) 5, 7, 9; 8, 4, 2; 1, 3, 6   (b) 2, 4, 9, 1, 3, 8; 6, 5, 7

(c) 5, 7, 8; 2, 4, 9; 1, 3, 6   (d) 1, 2, 3; 4, 5, 6; 7, 8, 9

Sol. (c) Considering option (c); 5, 7, 8 are figures composed of one straight lines. 2, 4, 9 are figures composed of two straight lines and 1, 3, 6 are figures composed of three straight lines. Hence, option (c) is correct.

⏰ Let's Practice

1. Find the figure in the place of question mark.

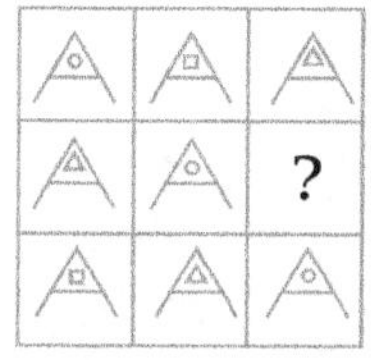
(a) 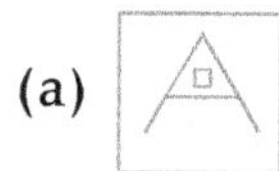
(b) 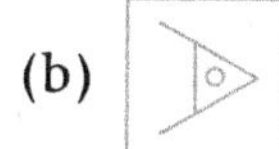
(c) 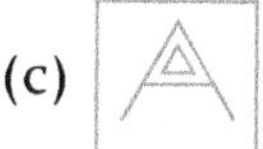
(d) 

2. Select the figures below carefully and find the missing figure represented by question mark (?).

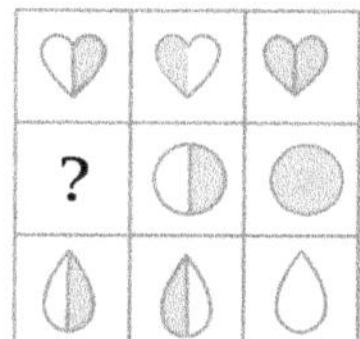
(a) 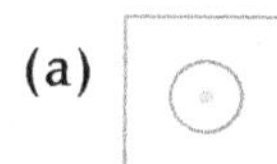
(b) 
(c) 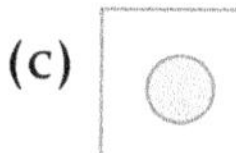
(d) 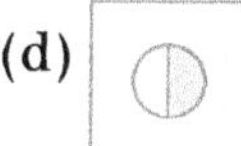

3. Find the figure in place of question mark.

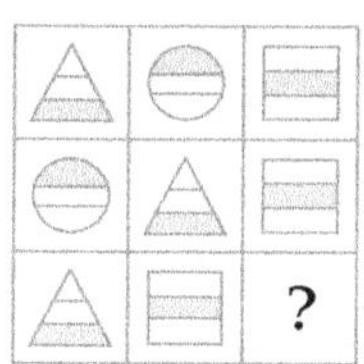
(a) 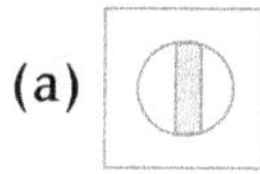
(b) 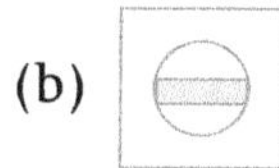
(c) 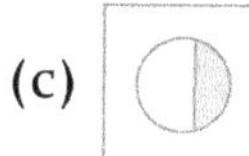
(d) 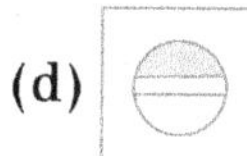

4. Find the figure in place of question mark.

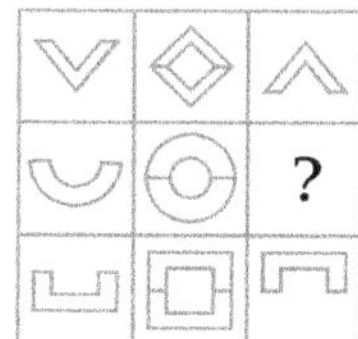
(a) 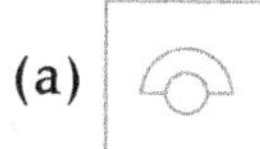
(b) 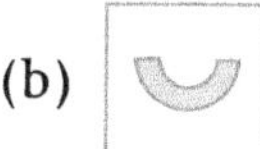
(c) 
(d) 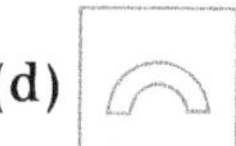

5. Find the number in place of question mark.

2	42	10
30	4	50
8	28	?

(a) 19   (b) 21   (c) 6   (d) 15

Directions (Q.Nos. 6-8) Group the given figures into three classes using each figure only once.

6.

(a) 1, 5, 7; 3, 4, 9; 2, 6, 8   (b) 1, 5, 7; 3, 4, 8; 2, 6, 9
(c) 3, 4, 9; 1, 5, 8; 6, 7, 9   (d) 3, 6, 9; 1, 5, 9; 2, 4, 8

7.

(a) 2, 3, 8; 1, 5, 9; 4, 6, 7   (b) 1, 4, 5; 2, 3, 9; 5, 6, 7
(c) 1, 5, 8; 2, 3, 9; 4, 6, 7   (d) 2, 3, 9; 4, 6, 8; 1, 5, 7

8.

(a) 2, 3, 5; 1, 4, 6; 7, 8, 9   (b) 1, 2, 4; 3, 9, 9; 5, 7, 8
(c) 1, 2, 4; 3, 5, 7; 6, 8, 9   (d) 1, 2, 3; 4, 5, 6; 6, 7, 8

9. Group the given numbers into three classes using each number only once.

12÷6	10–5	2×1
1	2	3
3×1	2+1	40÷8
4	5	6
0+5	6÷2	4–2
7	8	9

(a) 1, 3, 9; 2, 6, 7; 4, 5, 8   (b) 1, 4, 9; 2, 5, 7; 3, 6, 8
(c) 8, 7, 9; 5, 6, 3; 4, 2, 1   (d) 3, 2, 6; 7, 4, 5; 1, 8, 9

10. There are 15 Mangoes shown below :

How many groups of 5's can be formed from the group of mangoes?
(a) 6   (b) 3   (c) 10   (d) 3

Mirror Images

In 'Mirror image', the left part of an object appears right and right part appears left in a mirror. In this chapter you will learn how different objects are seen when they get reflected in mirror.

EXAMPLE 1 Andy kept his elephant toy in front of the mirror. How will it look like in the mirror?

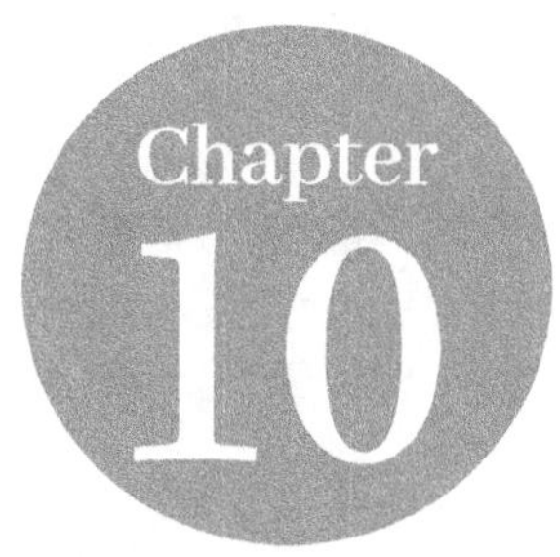

Sol. (d) The correct mirror image of the elephant toy is given in option (d) as shown in adjoining figure.

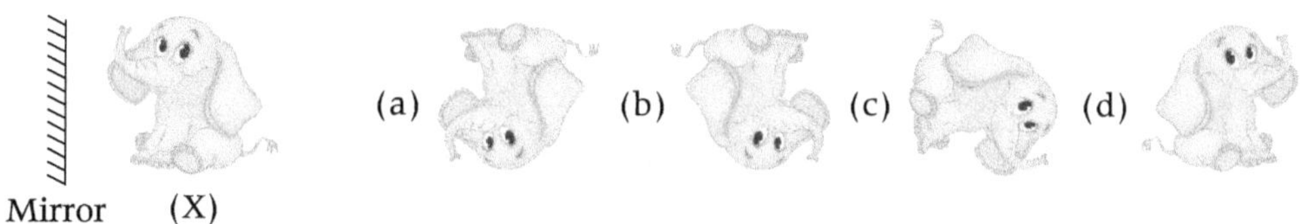

Hence, option (d) is correct.

EXAMPLE 2 The given below numbers are written on a wall. The mirror image of the numbers will be

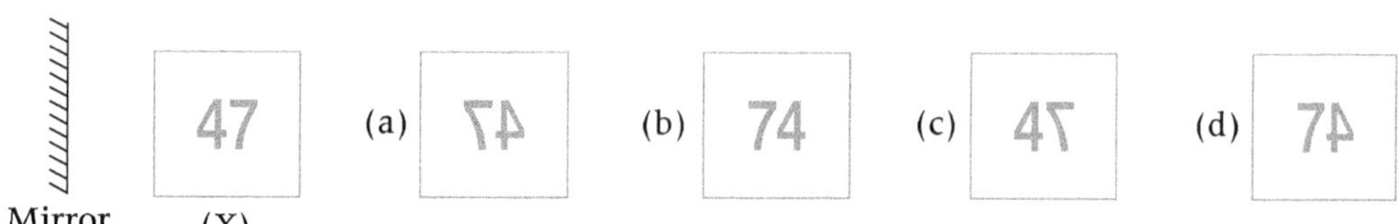

Sol. (a) The correct mirror image of the numbers is given in option (a) as shown below :

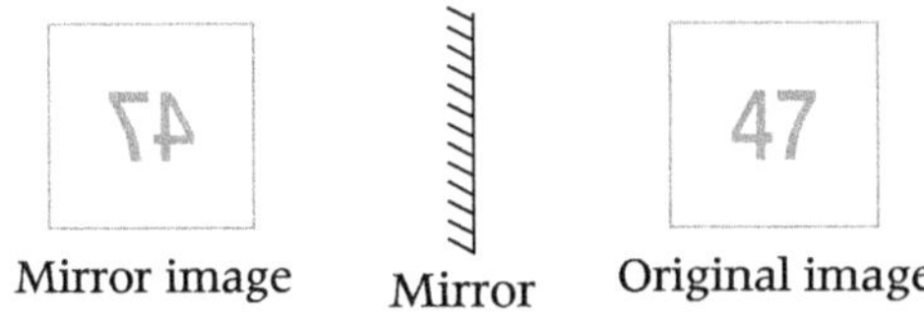

Mirror image   Mirror   Original image

Hence, option (a) is correct.

EXAMPLE 3   Two letters are written outside a shop. How the letters will appear in the side mirror of the car?

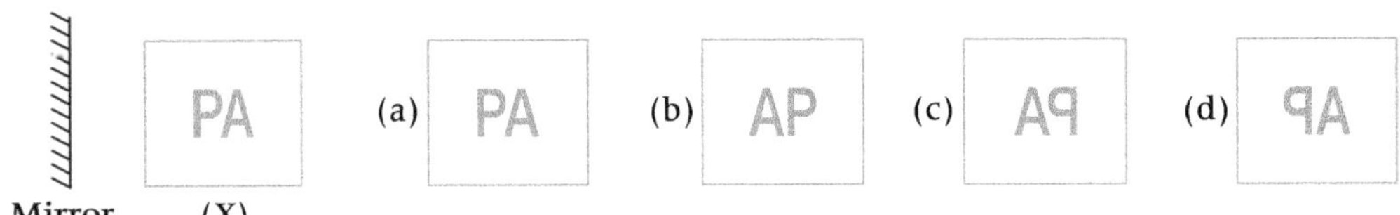

Mirror   (X)

Sol. (c) The two letters will appear in the side mirror of the car as given in option (c) as shown below :

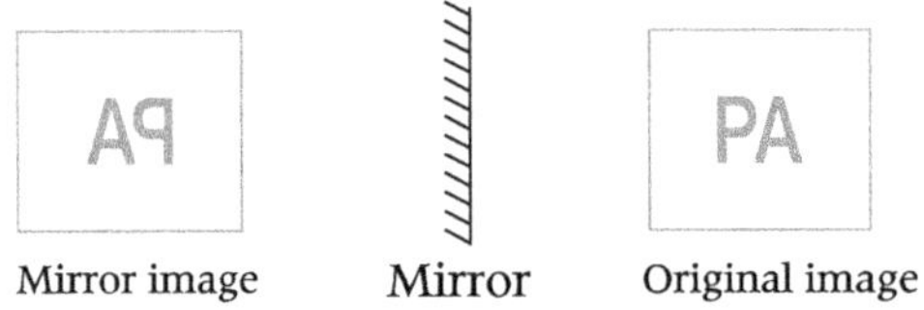

Mirror image   Mirror   Original image

Hence, option (c) is correct.

⏰ Let's Practice

1. A picture is drawn on a cardboard. What will be its mirror image?

(X)

2. Choose the correct mirror image of a dog standing beside the mirror.

(X)

3. Jake's photograph as shown below is kept on a table. What will be the mirror image of the photograph?

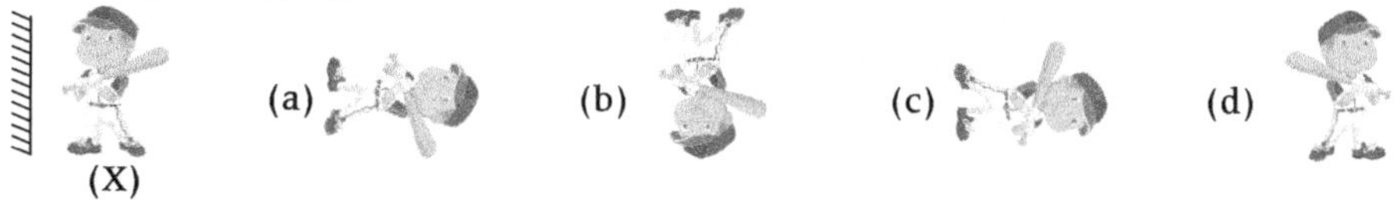

(a)   (b)   (c)   (d)

4. A child kept a toy in front of the mirror as shown below. How will it appear in the mirror?

(a)   (b)   (c)   (d)

5. Find the correct mirror image of the given figure (X).

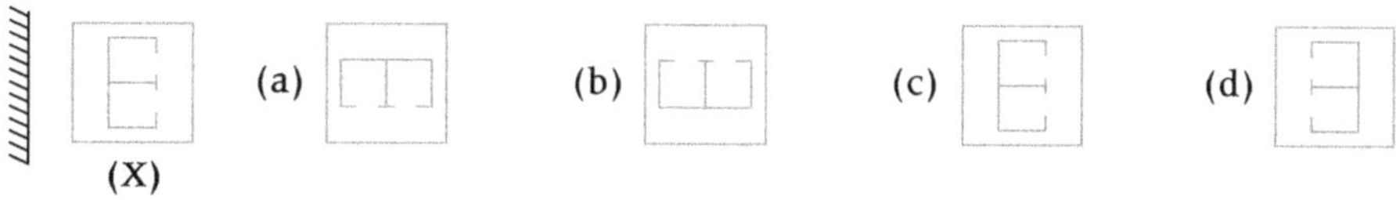

(a)   (b)   (c)   (d)

6. Find the mirror image of the numbers shown by the electronic meter.

(X) 81   (a) 18   (b) 8ᒋ   (c) 18   (d) ᒋ8

7. Harry is holding a card in his hand that is given. What will be the mirror image of the card?

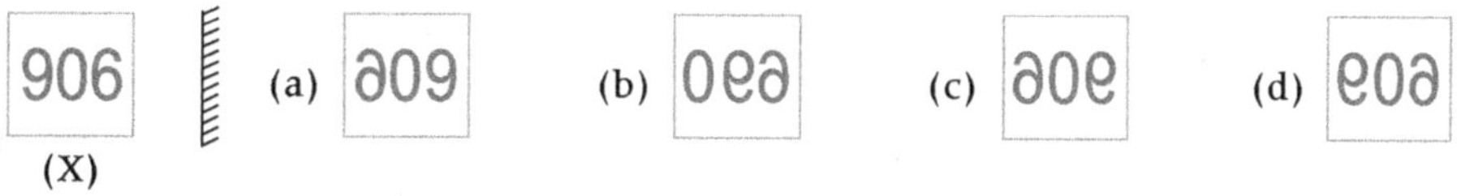

(X) 906   (a) ∂09   (b) 0e∂   (c) ∂0e   (d) e0∂

8. Choose the correct mirror image of the pattern shown below.

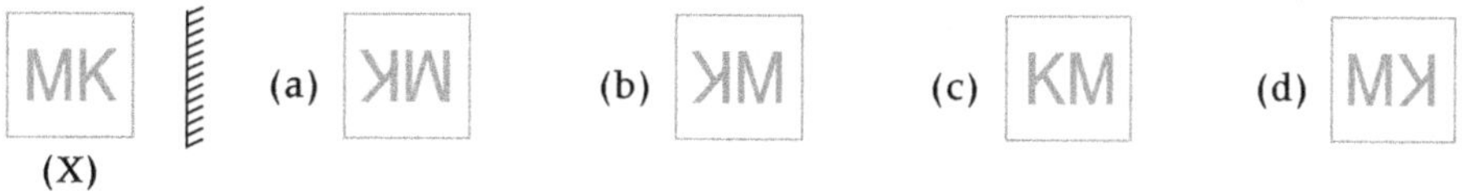

(X) MK   (a) ꓘM   (b) ꓘM   (c) KM   (d) MꓘM

9. Find the correct mirror image of the letters shown below :

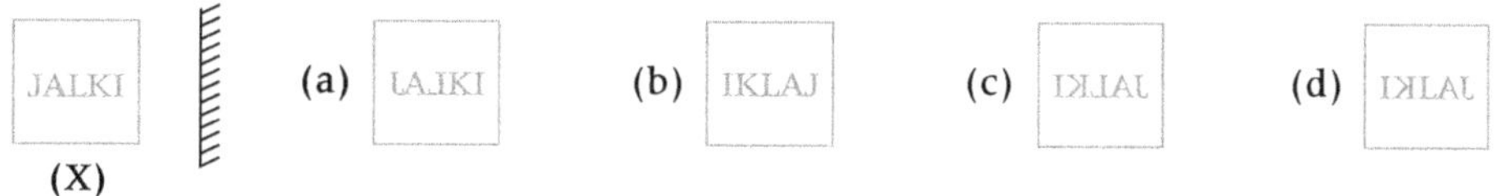

10. Find the correct mirror image of the word shown below :

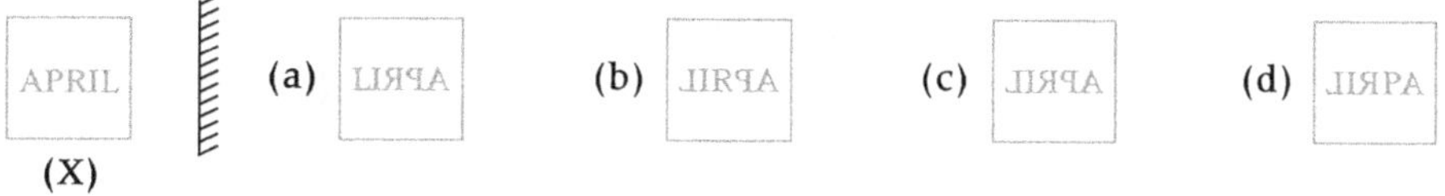

Position and Comparison Test

There are four positions, which can be understood with the help of the given diagram.

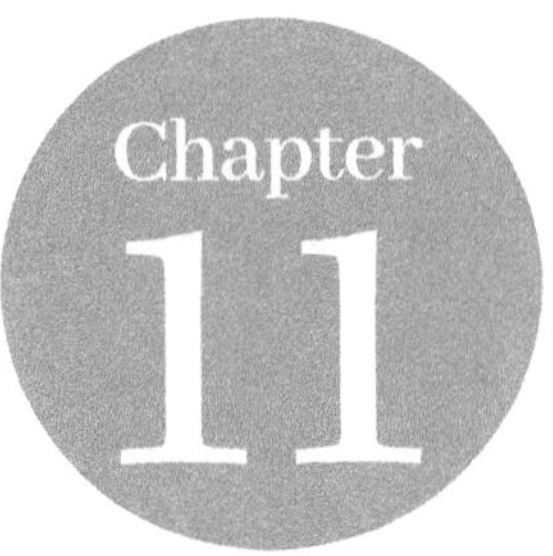

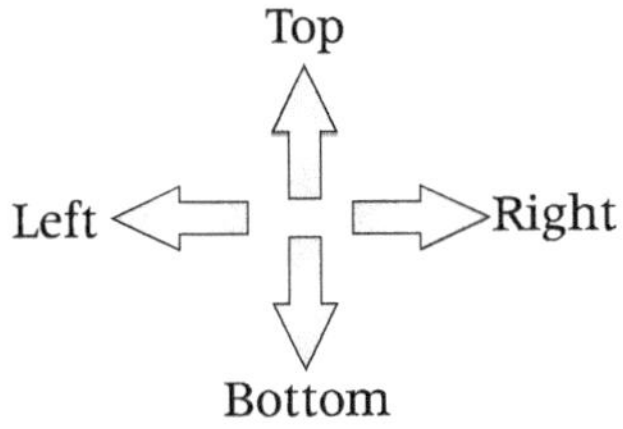

Types of questions covered in this chapter are as follow :

* Finding the position of an object from left, right, top or bottom.
* Find the object after interchanging the positions or removing of objects from the given sequence.

Directions (Ex. Nos. 1 and 2) In a toy shop some identical toy dolls are kept in a way as shown below. Observe them and answer the questions that follow.

EXAMPLE 1 Doll E is at what position from the left end?

    (a) 4th   (b) 5th   (c) 3th   (d) 6th

EXAMPLE 2 Doll B is at what position from the right end?

    (a) 6th   (b) 7th   (c) 3rd   (d) 5th

Sol. (Ex. Nos. 1 and 2)

1. (b) It is clear from the given arrangement of dolls that doll E is at 5th position from the left end.

$$\begin{array}{c}\text{A B C D E F G}\\ \text{Left} \xrightarrow{} \quad \text{Right}\\ \text{5th}\end{array}$$

Hence, option (b) is correct.

2. (a) Position of doll B from the right end is 6th when we count from the right end, i.e. from doll G to doll B.

$$\begin{array}{c}\text{A B C D E F G}\\ \text{Left} \xleftarrow{} \quad \text{Right}\\ \text{6th}\end{array}$$

Hence, option (a) is correct.

Note If end positions are not marked, then by default the positions are taken from our side.

Directions (Ex. Nos. 3 and 4) Observe the position of the toffees carefully and answer the questions based on them.

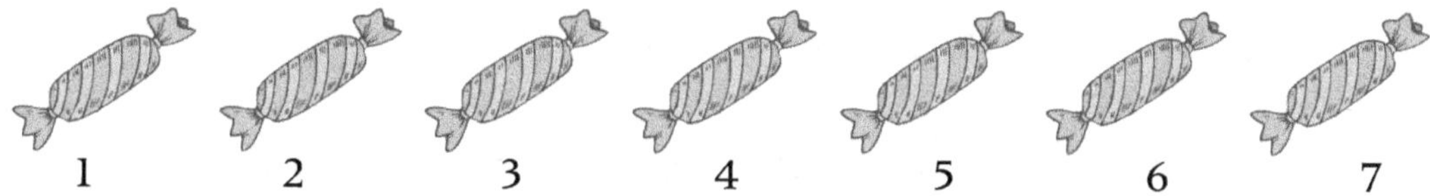

EXAMPLE 3 If toffee 3 is removed from the row, then how many toffees are there between toffee 2 and toffee 6?

   (a) 4   (b) 5   (c) 2   (d) 3

EXAMPLE 4 If the positions of toffee 2 and toffee 5 are interchanged, then which toffee is second to the left of toffee 2?

   (a) 5   (b) 3   (c) 6   (d) 1

Sol. (Ex. Nos. 3 and 4)

3. (c) There are two toffees between toffee 2 and toffee 6 when toffee 3 is removed and this can be shown as :

$$\begin{array}{c}1 \quad 2 \quad \cancel{3} \; \boxed{4 \quad 5} \; 6 \quad 7\\ \text{Left} \qquad\qquad\qquad \text{Right}\end{array}$$

So, 4 and 5 will be between toffee 2 and toffee 6. Hence, option (c) is correct.

4. (b) When toffee 2 and toffee 5 interchange its positions, then the positions of toffees can be shown as :

$$\begin{array}{c}1 \quad 5 \; \boxed{3} \; 4 \quad 2 \quad 6 \quad 7\\ \text{Left} \xleftarrow{} \quad \text{Right}\\ \text{2nd to the left}\end{array}$$

So, toffee 3 is second to the left of toffee 2. Hence, option (b) is correct.

EXAMPLE 5 In a race of four boys, Tany is ahead of Stephen, but behind Harper. Harper is between Jack and Tany. Who amongst the four won the race?

    (a) Stephen   (b) Tany   (c) Harper   (d) Jack

Sol. (a) The positions of the four participants can be shown as :

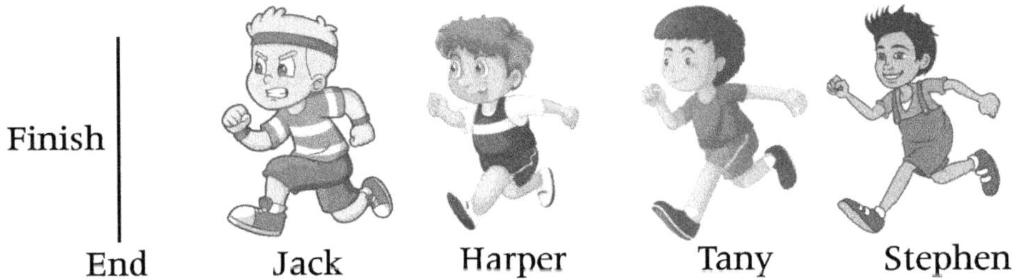

From the above positions of the boys, we can see that Jack won the race.

Hence, option (d) is correct.

⏰ Let's Practice

1. Some similar toys are hanging in a toy shop which are shown below.

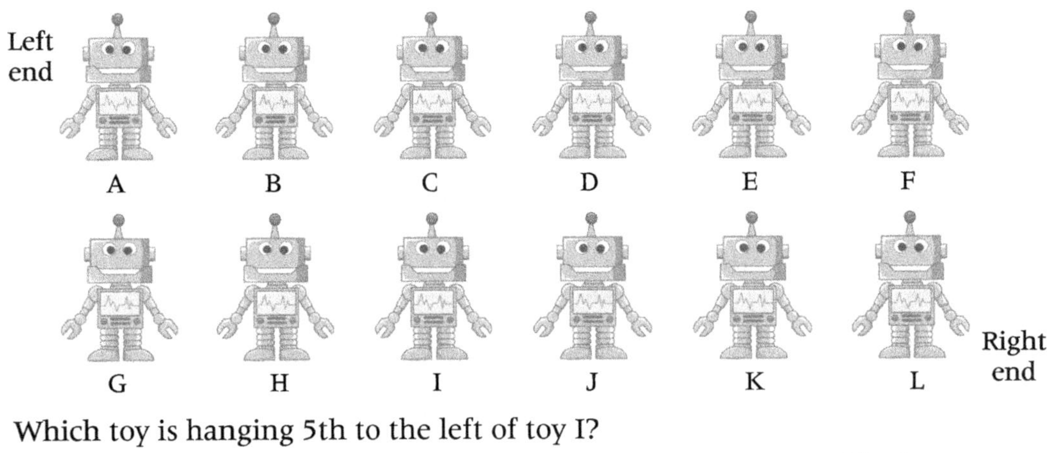

    Which toy is hanging 5th to the left of toy I?

    (a) E   (b) D   (c) C   (d) G

2. Seven books are arranged in a shelf as shown below and given the name as K, L, M, N, O, P and Q. If book M is at 3rd position from the top, then what is its position from the bottom?

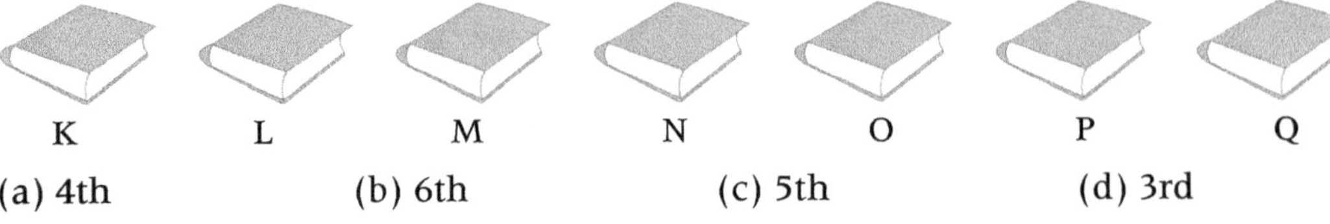

    (a) 4th   (b) 6th   (c) 5th   (d) 3rd

3. Which letter will be 5th from the Right end?

                Left   O X Q A E D G L W R Y   Right

(a) E   (b) G   (c) D   (d) W

Directions (Q. Nos. 4 and 5) Some trees are planted in a garden as shown below and named as P, Q, R, S, T, U and V. Now, answer the questions based on their positions.

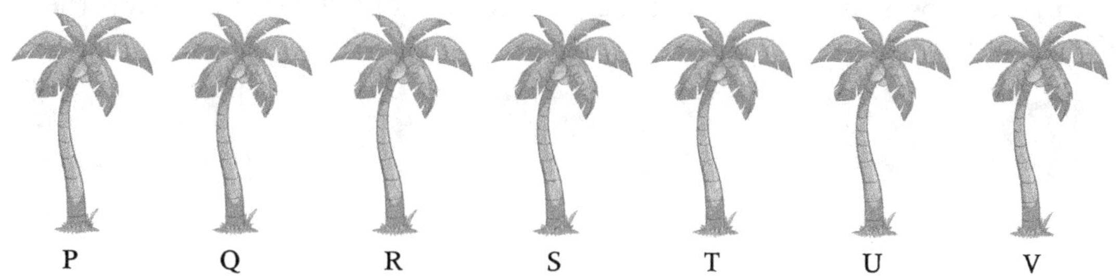

    P   Q   R   S   T   U   V

4. Tree S is between tree R and tree

(a) Q   (b) T   (c) U   (d) P

5. Which tree is 4th to the right of tree Q?

(a) S   (b) T   (c) U   (d) V

6. Some teddies are drawn on a wall as shown below and the letters represent their names. If the positions of F and J are interchanged, then which teddy is second to the left of F ?

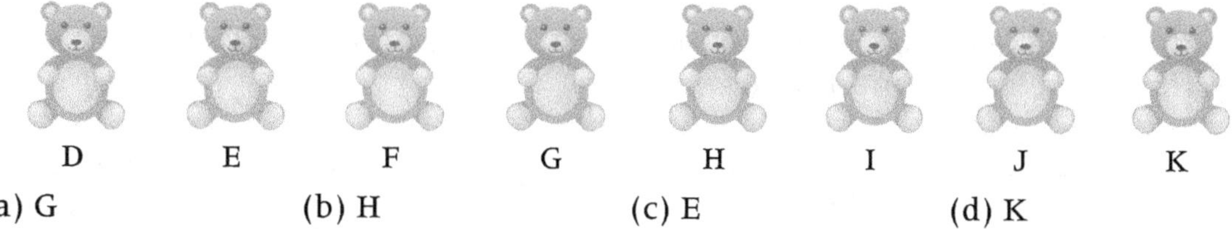

    D   E   F   G   H   I   J   K

(a) G   (b) H   (c) E   (d) K

Directions (Q. Nos. 7 and 8) Observe the given pictures carefully and answer the questions based on it.

7. How many boys between the boys on 2nd and 8th position?
   (a) 2   (b) 4   (c) 5   (d) 3

8. If boys on 2nd and 8th positions interchange their positions, then who is third to the right of 8th boy after interchanging the position?
   (a) 2nd boy   (b) 4th boy   (c) 5th boy   (d) 9th boy

Directions (Q. Nos. 9 and 10) Look at the arrangement of teddies and answer the questions that follow.

A   B   C   D   E   F   G

Left end   Right end

9. Which teddy is at 5th position from the right end?
   (a) B   (b) C
   (c) E   (d) D

10. If teddy F is removed from the arrangement, then which teddy is to the immediate left of teddy G?
    (a) C   (b) D
    (c) B   (d) E

11. If flowers 3 and 9 are removed from the arrangement, then how many flowers are there between 5th and 10th flower ?

Left end   1   2   3   4   5

6   7   8   9   10   Right end

(a) 2   (b) 4   (c) 3   (d) 5

Directions (Q. Nos. 12 and 13) Nine ice-cream cones are kept in a stand as shown below. Answer the questions based on their positions.

Left end   E   F   G   H   I   J   K   L   M   Right end

12. If one more ice-cream cone N is kept in a stand after M, then how many ice-cream cones are to the left of cone J?
    (a) 5   (b) 7
    (c) 6   (d) 3

13. If two ice-cream cones G and M are removed from stand, then which cone is in the middle of the stand?
    (a) K   (b) H
    (c) J   (d) I

Directions (Q. Nos. 14 and 15) Observe the given figure carefully and answer the questions based on it.

Left   T   U   V   W   X   Y   Z   Right

14. What is the position of Bat V from the left end?
    (a) First   (b) Third
    (c) Fourth   (d) Second

15. Which bat is in the middle of W and Y ?
    (a) T   (b) V
    (c) X   (d) Z

16. In an examination, Bob scored more than only Andy. Peter scored more than Bob but less than Herry. Who scored highest marks among these four?
    (a) Bob   (b) Harry
    (c) Peter   (d) Andy

Chapter 12

Find Direction

There are four main directions, whose names are East, West, North and South, which can be easily understood with the help of following diagram.

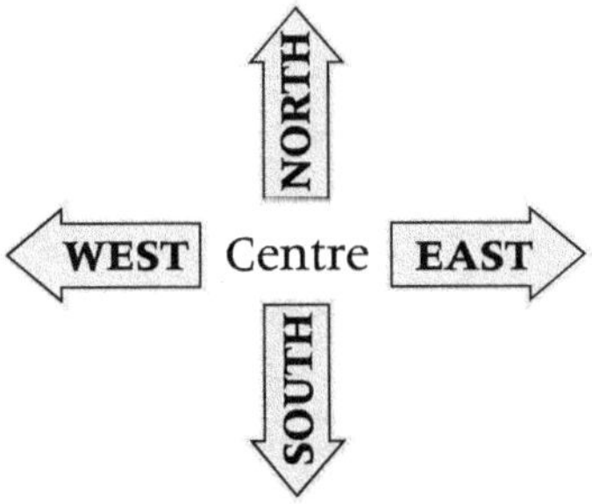

Directions (Ex. Nos. 1 and 2) Observe the positions of the trees in the garden and answer the questions that follow.

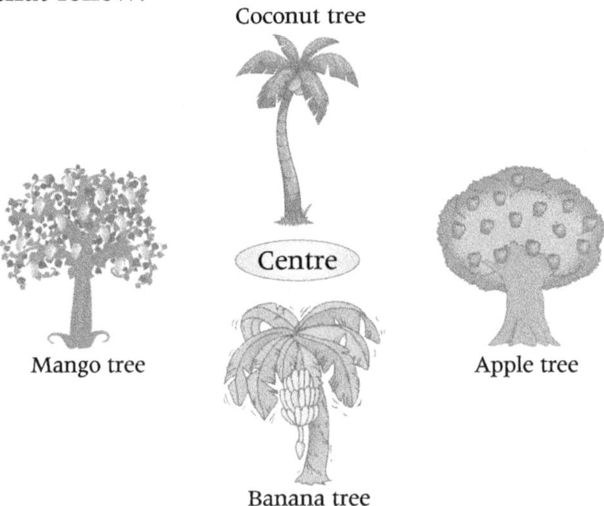

EXAMPLE 1 Which tree is in the East direction?

(a) Mango tree (b) Apple tree (c) Banana tree (d) Coconut tree

EXAMPLE 2 Banana tree is in which direction in the garden?

    (a) West   (b) North   (c) East   (d) South

Sol. (Ex. Nos. 1 and 2) The positions of trees can be shown as :

Coconut tree
(North)

Mango tree   **Centre**   Apple tree
(West)   (East)

Banana tree
(South)

  1. (b) From the above diagram it is clear that, apple tree is in the East direction. Hence, option (b) is correct.

  2. (d) From the above diagram it is clear that, banana tree is in the South direction according to its position in the garden. Hence, option (d) is correct.

⏰ Let's Practice

Directions (Q. Nos. 1 and 2) Observe the positions of House, Church, Grocery shop and Temple and then answer the questions that follow.

House

Centre

Grocery
shop   Church

Temple

  1. House is in which direction from the temple?

    (a) North   (b) East   (c) South   (d) West

  2. Which place is in the West direction?

    (a) House   (b) Church   (c) Grocery shop   (d) Temple

Directions (Q. Nos. 3 and 4) Observe the positions of toys kept in a toy shop and then answer the questions that follow.

3. Cat is in which direction from monkey?
   (a) North   (b) West   (c) South   (d) East

4. Which toy is in the North direction?
   (a) Kitty   (b) Monkey   (c) Cat   (d) Elephant

Directions (Q. Nos. 5 and 6) Four items are shown below. Observe them and then answer the questions based on them.

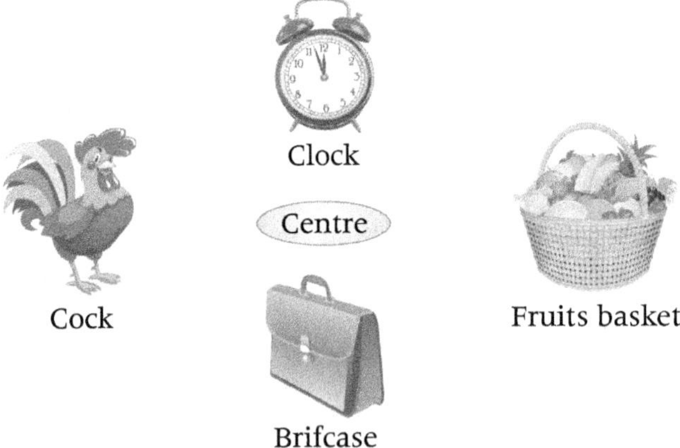

5. Which item is in the West direction?
   (a) Fruits basket   (b) Clock   (c) Briefcase   (d) Cock

6. Clock is in which direction from the briefcase?
   (a) North   (b) East   (c) South   (d) West

Directions (Q. Nos. 7 and 8) Read the map of India shown below and then answer the questions that follow.

7. Which place is in the South direction in the above map?
   (a) Madhya Pradesh (b) Bihar   (c) Punjab   (d) Kerala

8. Gujarat is in which direction from Jharkhand?
   (a) West   (b) South   (c) East   (d) North

Directions (Q. Nos. 9 and 10) Tom, Julia, Martin and Harry are playing a game and standing as shown below. Fill in the blanks based on their positions.

9. Martin is standing in .... direction.
   (a) North   (b) East   (c) South   (d) West

10. .... is standing in the East direction.
    (a) Harry   (b) Julia   (c) Tom   (d) Martin

Directions (Q. Nos. 11 and 12) Four trains are shown below. Observe them and then answer the questions based on them.

Train (A)

Centre

Train (C)

Train (B)

Train (D)

11. Which train is in the East direction?
    (a) Train A   (b) Train B   (c) Train C   (d) Train D

12. Train A is in which direction from the Train D?
    (a) East   (b) North   (c) West   (d) South

PRACTICE SET 01

1. If 'green' means 'white', 'white' means 'yellow' and 'yellow' means 'black', then what is the colour of milk ?

   (a) Green (b) White (c) Black (d) Yellow

2. Which of the answer figures is the right image of the given figure (X) ?

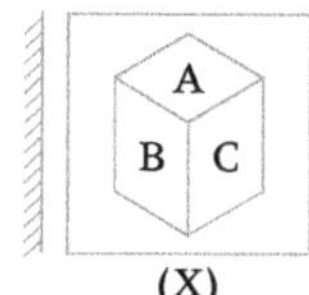

   (X)

(a) 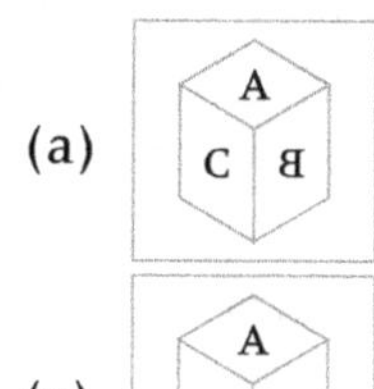 (b) 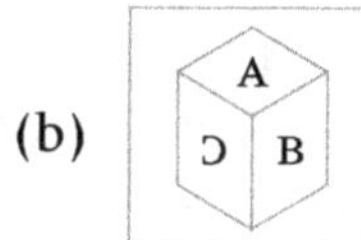

(c) (d) 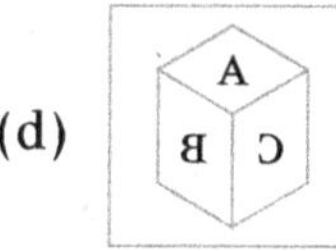

3. Which is the odd one out?

   (a) $10 + 9$ (b) 19×0 (c) $95 \div 5$ (d) $19 - 0$

4. Choose the correct option to complete the pattern.

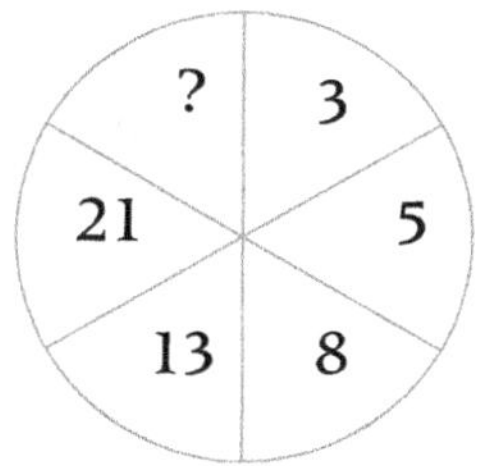

   (a) 1   (b) 26   (c) 34   (d) 45

Directions (Q. Nos. 5 and 6) Four boys are shown below, observe them and then answer the questions based on them.

5. Vishnu is in which direction?

   (a) East   (b) West
   (c) North   (d) South

6. Krishna is in which direction from the Ram?

   (a) South

   (b) North

   (c) West

   (d) East

7. Which pattern will complete the second pair in the same way as the first pair?

   6 : 18 :: 3 : ?

   (a) 9   (b) 10
   (c) 12   (d) 15

8. How many slant lines are in the given figure?

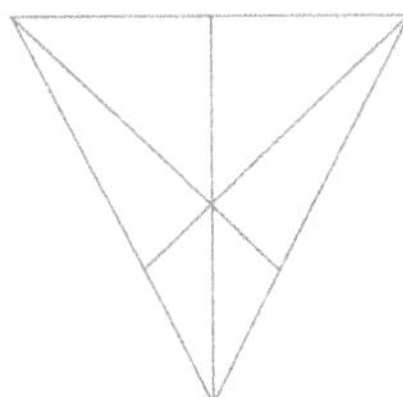

(a) 4   (b) 15   (c) 14   (d) 13

9. Find the figure in the place of question mark (?).

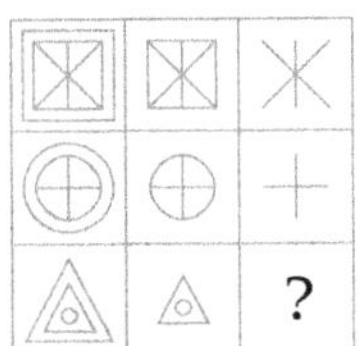

(a) 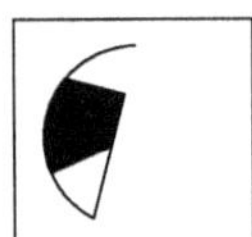   (b) 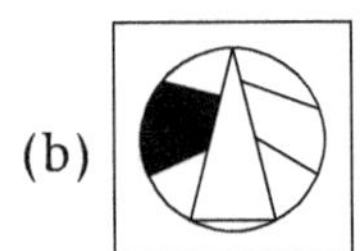

(c) 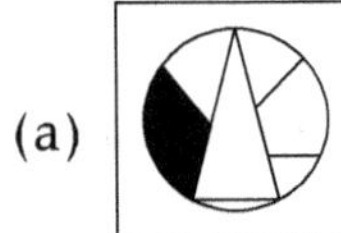   (d) 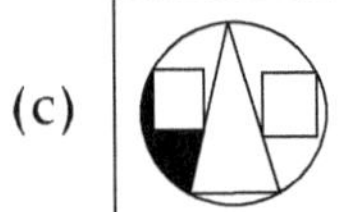

10. Find out the figure from the options that contains figure (X) as its part.

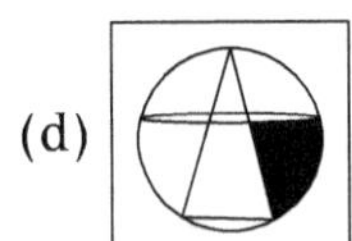

(a)   (b)

(c)   (d)

11. Identify the one that does not belong to the group.

(a) 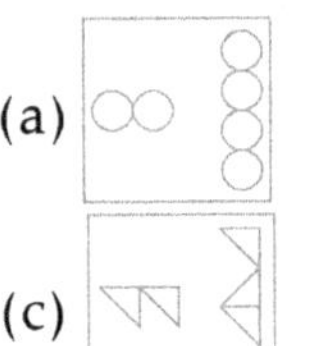   (b)

(c)   (d)

12. Which pair of letters will continue the series?

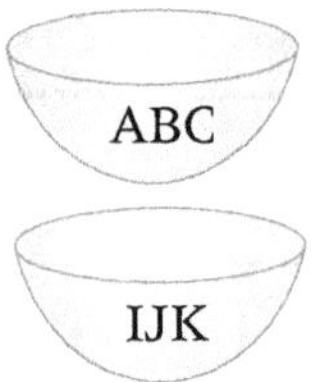 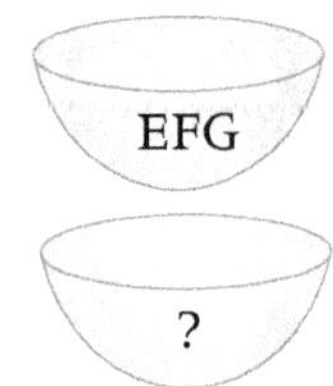

(a) LMN   (b) MNO   (c) KLM   (d) ONM

13. If in a certain code, LUTE is written as MUTE and FATE is written as GATE, then how will BLUE be written in that code?

(a) CLUE   (b) GLUE   (c) FLUE   (d) SLUE

14. Choose the correct combination of numbers, so that letters when arrange from a meaningful word.

R   E   T   T   E   L

1   2   3   4   5   6

(a) 654321   (b) 234651
(c) 345612   (d) 125643

15. Some letters shown below in each box are related to each other. Find the missing letters.

CG : EI   ::   FJ : ?

(a) LM   (b) IJ   (c) GK   (d) HL

16. How many oval shapes are there in the given image?

(a) 2   (b) 5   (c) 6   (d) 8

17. What will be the mirror image of given figure (X) ?

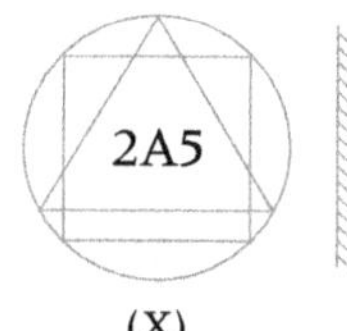

(X)

(a) 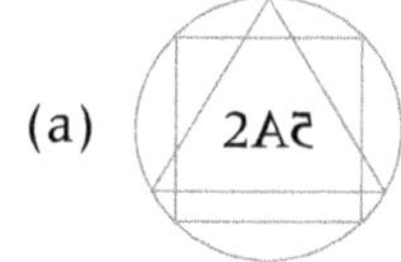   (b)

(c)    (d)

18. Choose the figure from the given alternatives that will complete the given figure.

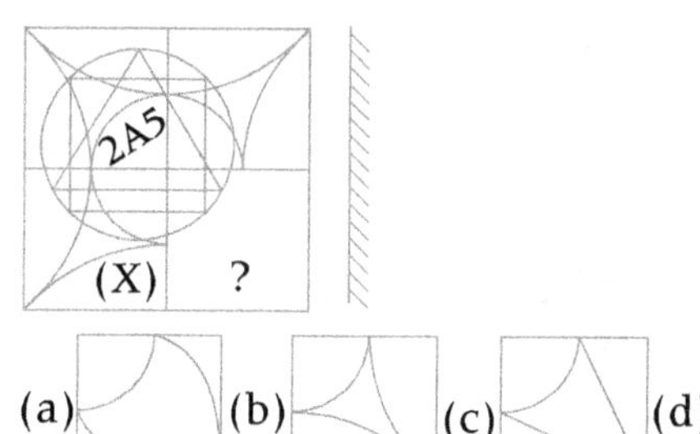

(a)   (b)   (c)   (d)

19. Which letters from the given alternatives when replaced with question mark (?) will form one name of subject and one name of animal?

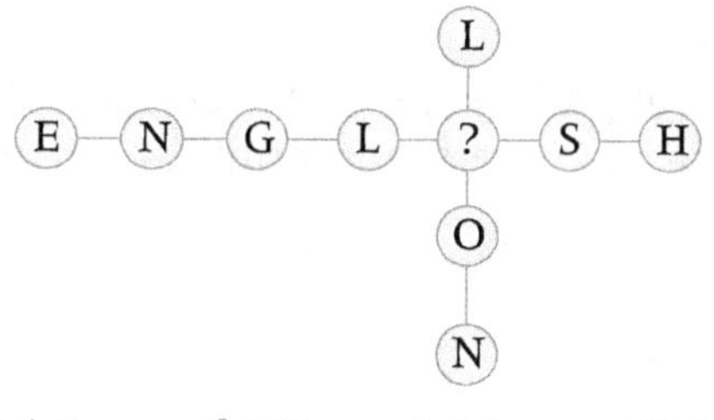

(a) G   (b) H   (c) I   (d) J

Directions (Q. Nos. 20 and 21) Study the table and answer the following questions.

Figures	Codes	Figures	Codes
	A		B
	M		G
	O		W

20. What is the code of  ?

(a) AO   (b) OW   (c) WO   (d) GB

21. What is the code of  ?

(a) MG   (b) AB   (c) OG   (d) BW

22. Find the figure from the option which is hidden in figure (X).

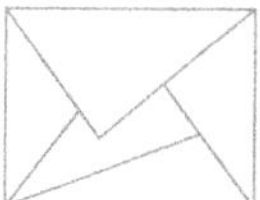

(a) 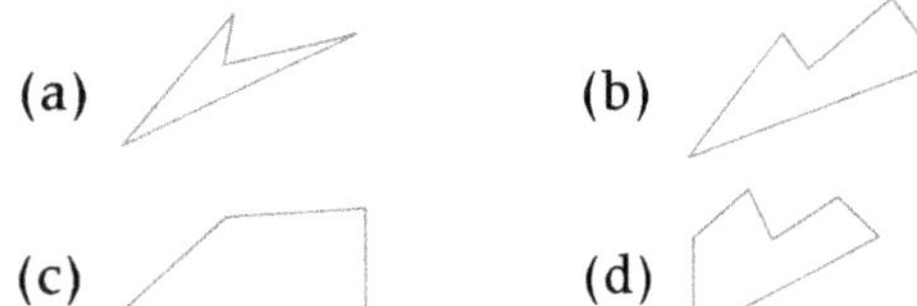   (b)

(c)   (d)

23. Group of the given letters into three classes using each number only once.

3	4	1
7	6	5
11	8	9

(a) 1, 2, 3; 4, 5, 6; 7, 8, 9
(b) 1, 4, 7; 2, 5, 8; 3, 6, 9
(c) 4, 2, 6; 1, 7, 3; 5, 8, 9
(d) 9, 4, 1; 2, 6, 7; 3 ,5, 8

24. What comes next in the pattern?

(a) 25   (b) 24   (c) 22   (d) 23

25. Which pair of letters does not belong to the group?

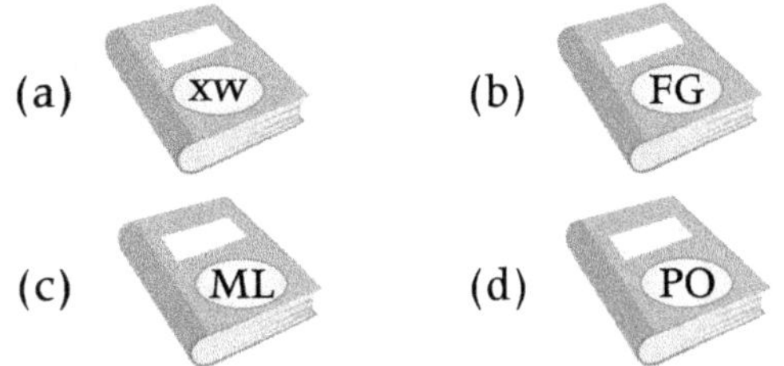

(a) XW   (b) FG

(c) ML   (d) PO

26. In the following options, find the word that can be made from the letters of the given word.

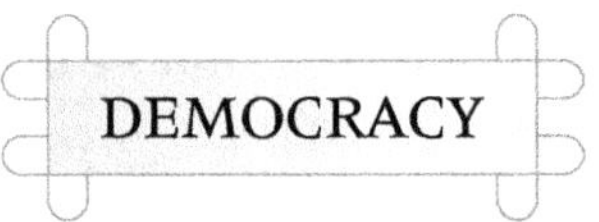

(a) SECRECY   (b) MICRO
(c) MARCY   (d) DEMON

27. Which of the answer figures is exactly the mirror image of the given figure (X)?

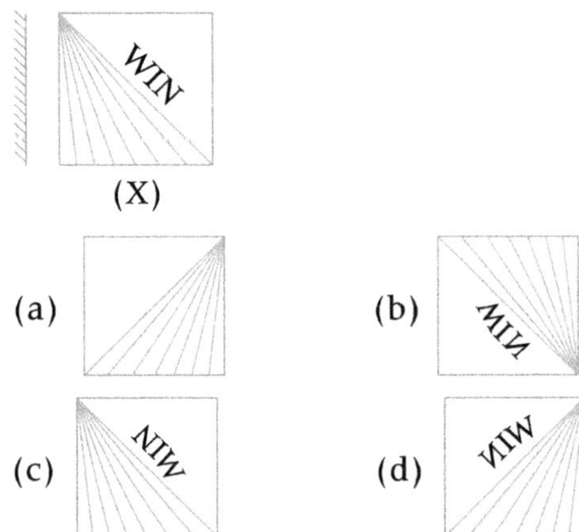

Directions (Q. Nos. 28 and 29) Observe the figure given below and answer the following questions.

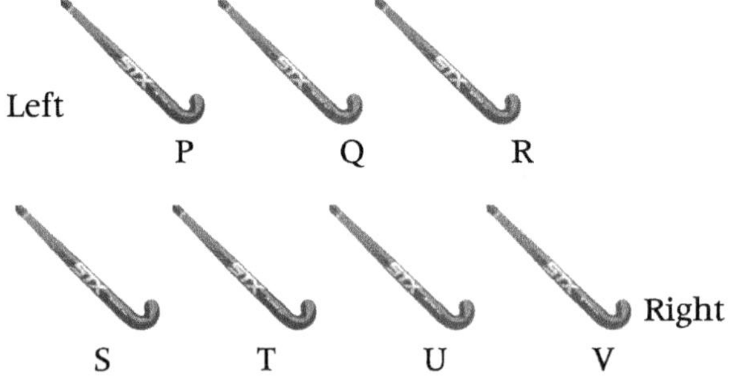

28. If S and T is removed from the series, then the Hockey ...... is in the middle.

(a) R   (b) U   (c) S   (d) P

29. Which Hockey lies in the middle of S and U ?
(a) P   (b) Q
(c) R   (d) T

30. Find the missing figure in the following pattern.

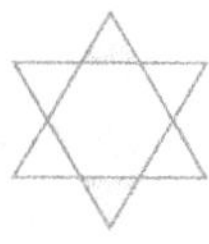 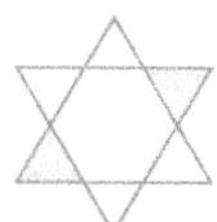 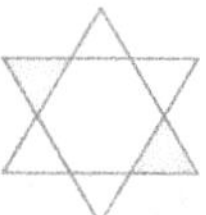

 **?** 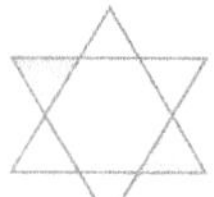

(a)    (b) 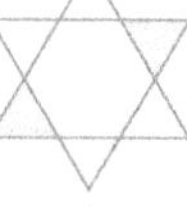

(c)    (d)

31. How many triangles are there in the butterfly given below ?

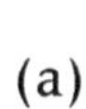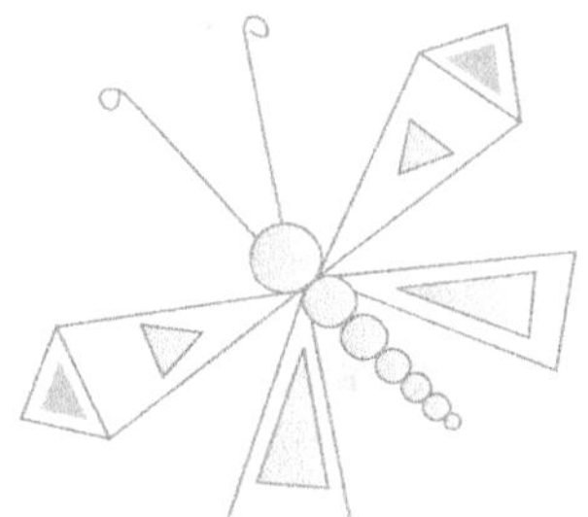

(a) 9   (b) 13   (c) 15   (d) 12

32. In which of the following alphabets is not embedded in figure (X).

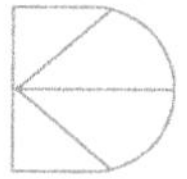

(a) O   (b) P   (c) R   (d) D

33. Which pattern below completes the second pair in the same way as the first pair?

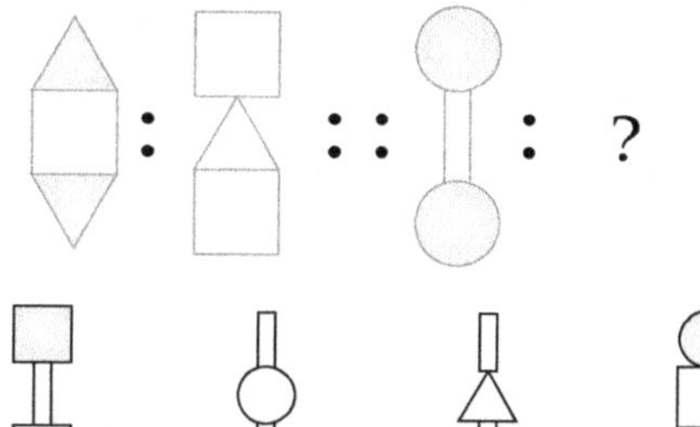

(a)   (b)   (c)   (d)

34. In which of the following series, the number of letters skipped between adjacent letters is same?
(a) ABEI   (b) DFJO   (c) FCZW   (d) LPQT

35. Find the missing number in the given pattern.

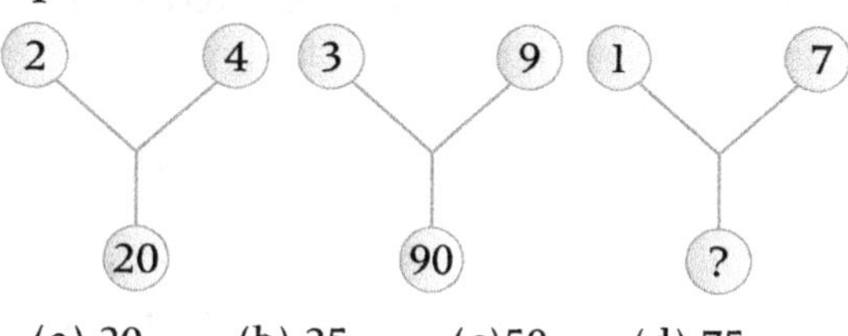

(a) 20   (b) 25   (c) 50   (d) 75

Answers

1. (d)	2. (c)	3. (b)	4. (c)	5. (b)	6. (a)	7. (a)	8. (a)	9. (d)	10. (b)
11. (c)	12. (b)	13. (a)	14. (a)	15. (d)	16. (c)	17. (c)	18. (b)	19. (c)	20. (b)
21. (a)	22. (b)	23. (b)	24. (b)	25. (b)	26. (c)	27. (d)	28. (a)	29 (d)	30. (b)
31. (d)	32. (a)	33. (b)	34. (c)	35 (c)					

PRACTICE SET  02

1. Identify the one that does not belong to the group.
   - (a) Friday
   - (b) Monday
   - (c) Wednesday
   - (d) Today

2. Figures in the first pair are related to each other in a certain way. Find the missing figure in the second pair in the same way as the first pair.

   △ : ☐ : ⌂ : ?

   (a) ◇   (b) ☐   (c) ⬡   (d) ⬡

3. Which letter from the given alternatives will complete the first word and start the second word?

   | P | A | G | ? | A | C | H |

   (a) S   (b) T   (c) E   (d) R

4. If Yellow is called Red, Red is called Blue, then what is the colour of Sunflower?
   - (a) Red   (b) Blue   (c) Black   (d) Pink

5. Four friends took part in a Maths olympiad. Tipsy scored more than Mark, but less than Ginny. Ginny does not scored the highest marks. Rax scored more than Tipsy. Who among them scored the least?
   - (a) Ginny   (b) Rax   (c) Tipsy   (d) Mark

Directions (Q. Nos. 6 and 7) Observe the positions of teddies and answer the questions that follow.

A   B   C   D   E   F   G   H

6. If teddy E is removed from the sequence, then which teddy is third to the left of G?
   - (a) D   (b) C   (c) B   (d) A

7. If one more teddy I is added after H in the sequence, then how many teddies are there after F ?
   - (a) 5   (b) 2   (c) 4   (d) 3

8. Find the number which come in place of question mark(?).

   14   21   28   ?

   - (a) 35   (b) 29
   - (c) 32   (d) 40

9. Count the number of rectangles in the figure shown below.

   - (a) 8   (b) 7
   - (c) 6   (d) 10

10. Find the mirror image of the given figure shown below.

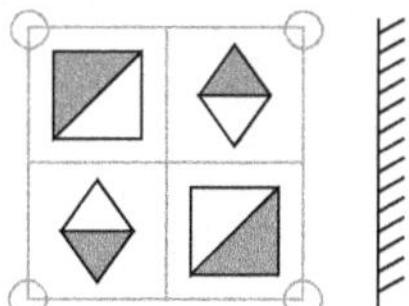

(a) 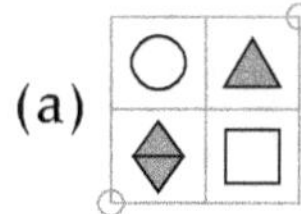   (b) 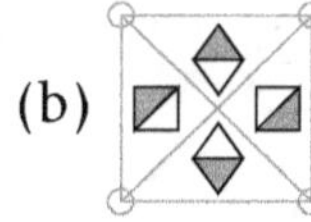

(c) 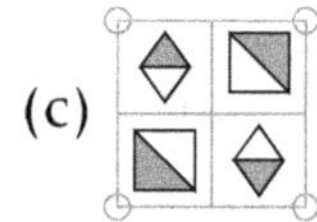   (d) 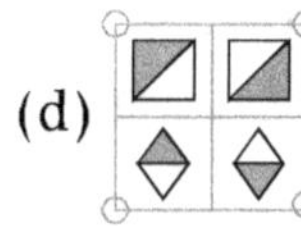

11. Which number from the given options will replace the question mark (?)?

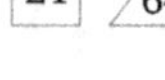  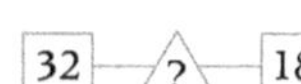

(a) 48   (b) 45
(c) 40   (d) 50

12. A pattern is drawn on a piece of paper. Which figure from the given alternatives will complete the given pattern?

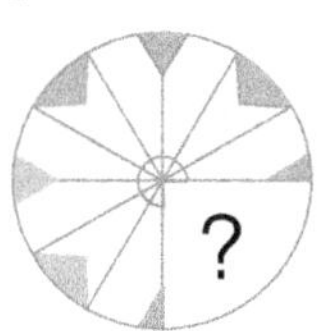

(a) 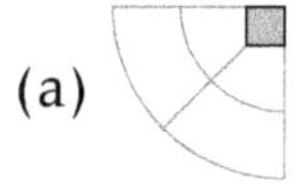   (b) 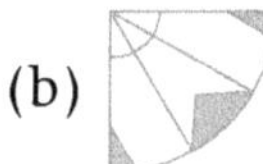

(c) 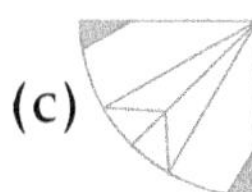   (d) 

13. In which figure the given shape (X) is hidden?

(X)

(a) 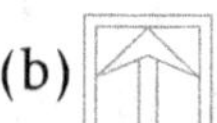 (b) (c) (d) 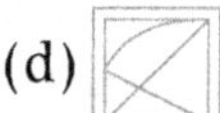

14. Which word from the given alternatives cannot be formed using the letters of the given word?

(a) NICE   (b) CHIN
(c) EACH   (d) THREAD

15. In the shop of a fruits vendor, fruits are kept as shown below :

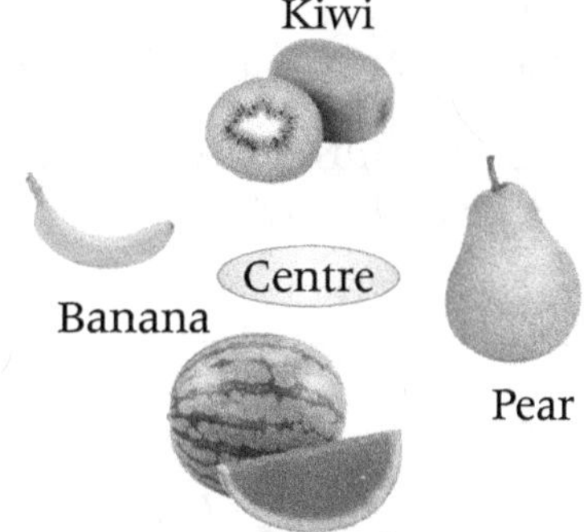

Which fruit is kept in the North direction?

(a) Banana   (b) Kiwi
(c) Pear   (d) Watermelon

16. TURN is related to URN, as FLITE is related to

(a) LITE   (b) TILE
(c) ELIT   (d) FILT

17. Arrange the given letters to form a meaningful word and then find its number arrangement.

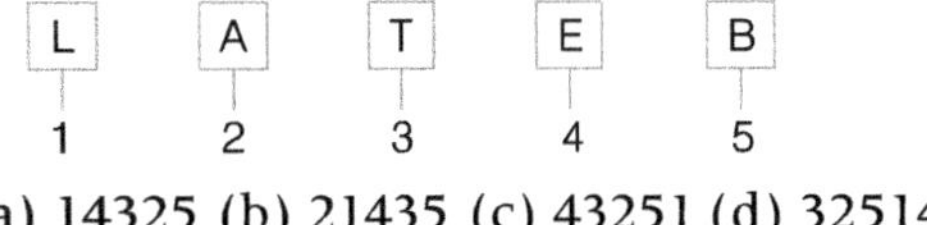

(a) 14325 (b) 21435 (c) 43251 (d) 32514

Direction (Q. No. 18) Below are given some pictures. Observe their directions and answer the questions that follows.

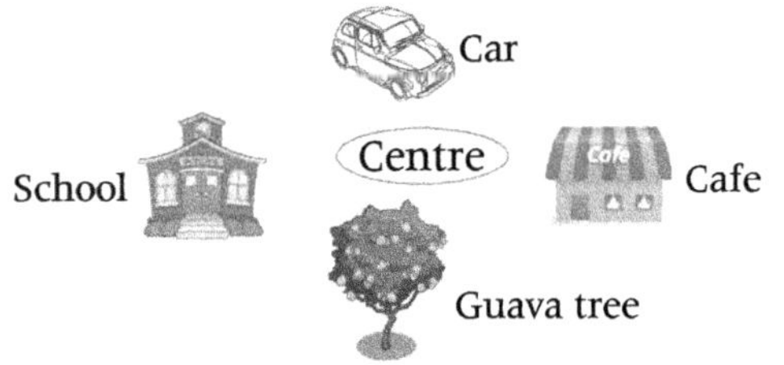

18. Cafe is in which direction in the above picture?

(a) North (b) East   (c) South (d) West

19. What is the mirror image of the letters given below?

(a) 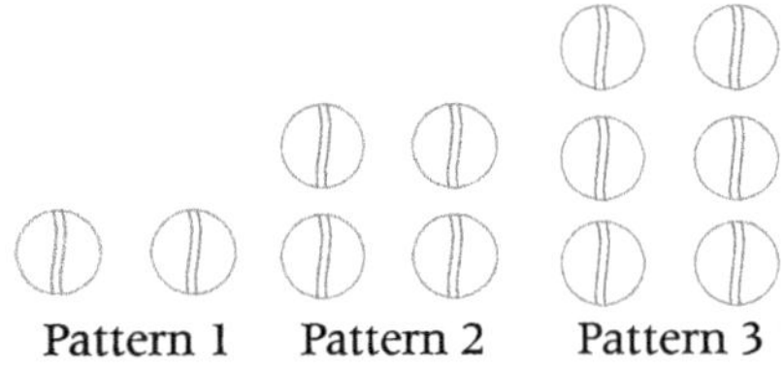   (b)   (c)   (d)

20. Some balls are shown following some pattern

Pattern 1   Pattern 2   Pattern 3

How many balls are there in the pattern 5?

(a) 10   (b) 8   (c) 7   (d) 12

21. In a certain code, 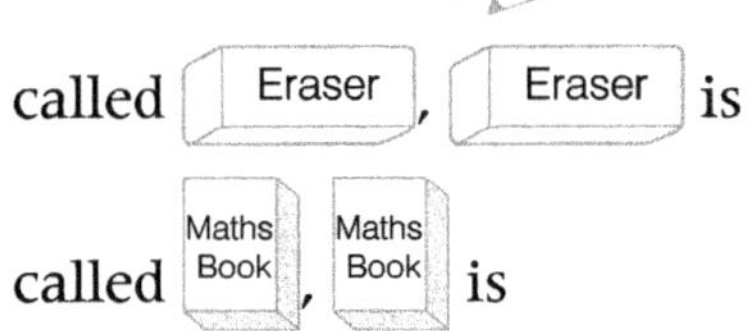 is called

called [Eraser], [Eraser] is

called 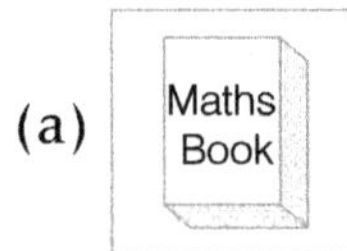 [Maths Book], 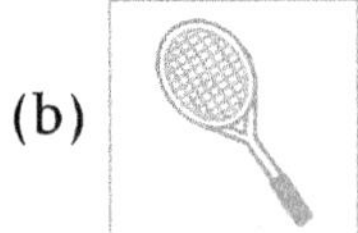 [Maths Book] is

called 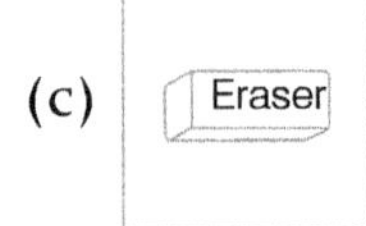 and 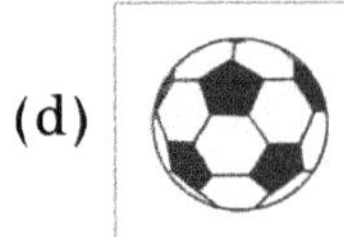 is called,

then what is used to write the text?

(a) 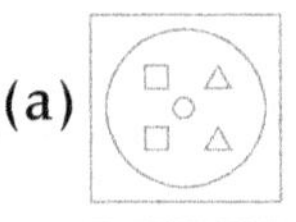 [Maths Book]   (b) 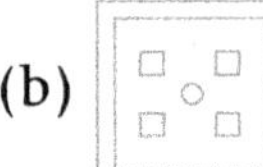

(c) 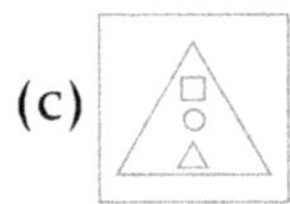 [Eraser]   (d) 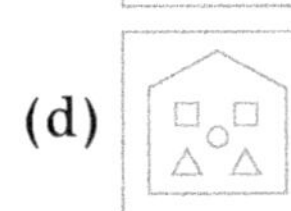

22. Which one is different?

(a)   (b)   (c)   (d)

23. Count the number of circles in the figure shown below.

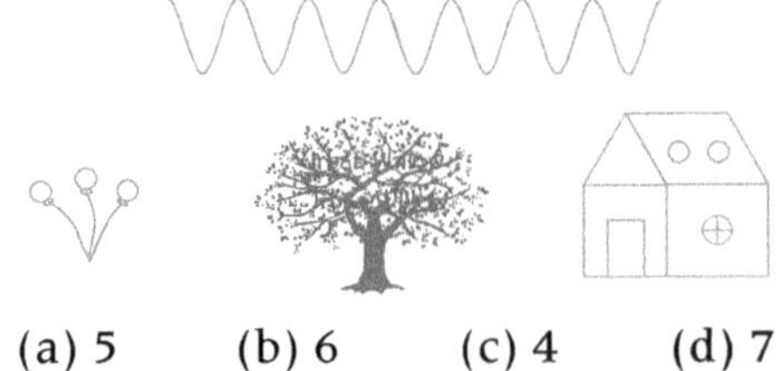

(a) 5   (b) 6   (c) 4   (d) 7

24. Which part from the given alternatives is hidden in the given figure(X)?

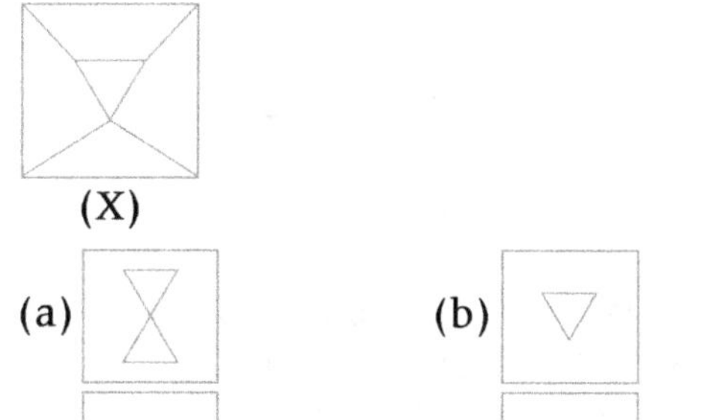

(X)

(a)   (b)

(c)   (d)

25. Which word from the given options can be formed using the letters of the given word?

MATHEMATICS

(a) RATE (b) STICK (c) STATE (d) HEAR

26. Find the missing number.

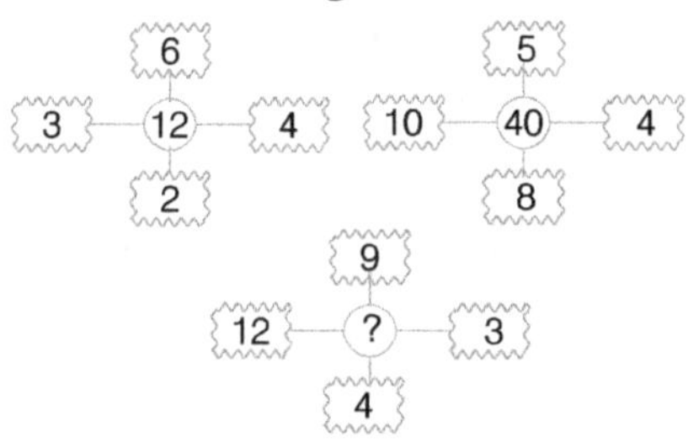

(a) 30   (b) 15   (c) 13   (d) 36

27. Complete the pattern given below by using the figures in the options.

△	△△	△△△
○○	○○○	○○○○
▭▭	?	⊞

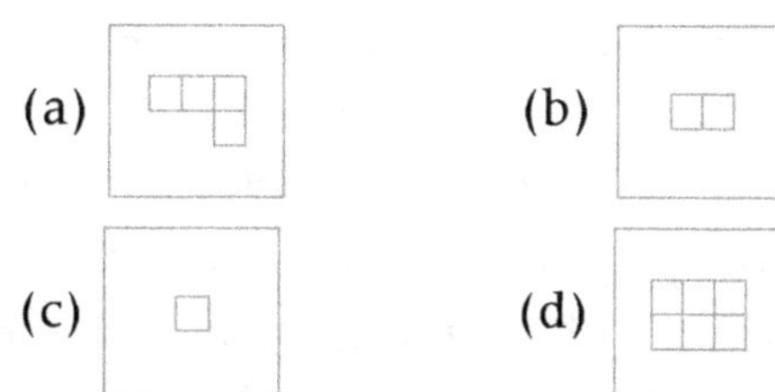

(a)   (b)

(c)   (d)

28. Figure in the first pair are related to each other in a certain way. Find the missing pair in the second pair in the same way as the first pair.

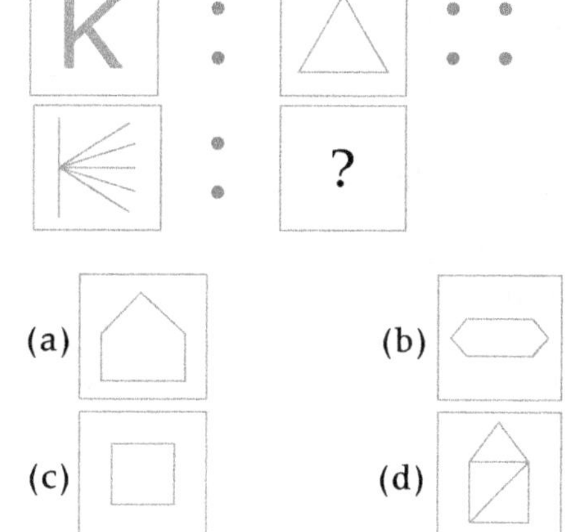

(a)   (b)

(c)   (d)

Direction (Q. No. 29) Below are given some cars. Observe their directions and answer the questions that follow.

29. Audi is in which direction from the Duster?

(a) North (b) East (c) South (d) West

30. In which of the following series, the number of letters skipped between adjacent letters in same?

(a) TZBC   (b) QSUW

(c) AFEG   (d) ADIJ

31. How many squares are there in the given figure?

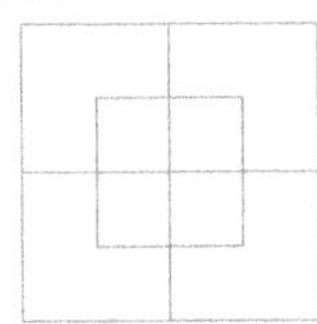

(a) 7   (b) 9   (c) 8   (d) 10

32. Which of the following options will complete the figure (X)?

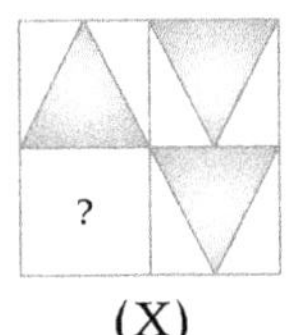

(X)

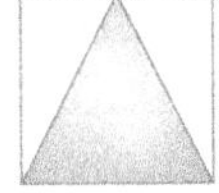 (a)   (b) 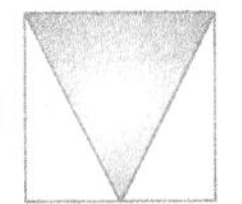

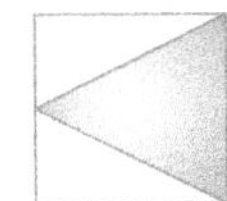 (c)   (d) 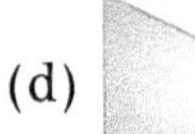

33. Group of the given numbers into three classes using each number only once.

3	35	8
1	2	3
25	4	21
4	5	6
2	5	9
7	8	9

(a) 7, 5, 3; 1, 9, 6; 8, 4, 2

(b) 7, 1, 8; 5, 9, 4; 3, 6, 2

(c) 3, 1, 6; 7, 5, 9; 4, 8, 2

(d) 2, 5, 3; 4, 6, 7, 1, 8, 9

34. A letter's series is shown below. Find the pair of letters that will continue the series.

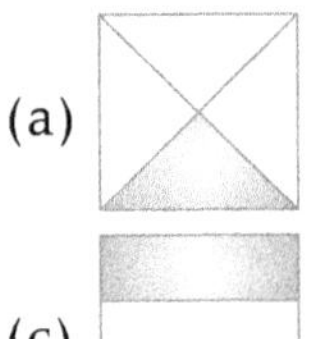

(a) MN   (b) PO   (c) OT   (d) PU

35. Which one is different from the given alternatives.

(a)   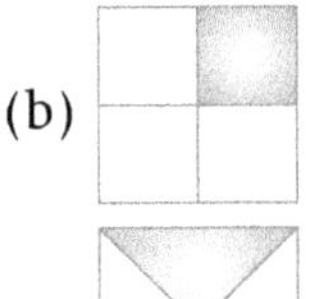 (b)

(c)    (d)

Answers

1. (d)	2. (c)	3. (c)	4. (a)	5. (d)	6. (b)	7. (d)	8. (a)	9. (b)	10. (c)
11. (d)	12. (b)	13. (a)	14. (d)	15. (b)	16. (a)	17. (d)	18. (b)	19. (a)	20. (a)
21. (c)	22. (c)	23. (b)	24. (b)	25. (c)	26. (d)	27. (a)	28. (b)	29. (a)	30. (b)
31. (d)	32. (a)	33. (a)	34. (d)	35. (c)					

Hints & Solutions

1. Matching Pairs

1. *(b)* As, lock and key are used together. In the same way, needle and thread are used together.

2. *(a)* As, ice-cream cone is of cone shape. In the same way, dice face is of square shape.

3. *(c)* In the first pair of figures, two slanting lines are added in the middle of the first figure to get the second figure.

Similarly, in the second pair, two slanting lines must be added in the middle part of the first figure to get the second figure.

So, figure in option (c) will complete the second pair.

4. *(b)* In the first pair of figures, first figure is divided into two parts and its right part is shown as the second figure with three circles in it.

Similarly, the rectangle should be divided into two parts and its right part must be shown as the second figure with three circles in it.

So, figure in option (b) is the missing figure.

5. *(c)* In the first pair, first figure is pointing upwards and second figure is pointing downwards, but the lines are different at the end.

Similarly, in the second pair, the second figure must be point downwards and the line at the end must be same as that of second figure in the first pair.

So, figure in option (c) will complete the pattern.

6. *(b)* As, $4 \times 2 = 8$, similarly $7 \times 2 = \boxed{14}$

So, number in the fourth balloon should be '14'.

7. *(b)* As, $10 + 10 = 20$, similarly $50 + 10 = \boxed{60}$

So, the price of fourth ice-cream is ₹ 60.

8. (b) As $58 \div 2 \Rightarrow 29$

Similarly, $86 \div 2 \Rightarrow \boxed{43}$

So, '43' will come in place of question mark. Hence, option (b) is correct.

9. (a) As, M N $\longrightarrow$ N M

Similarly, O Q $\longrightarrow$ $\boxed{Q\,O}$

So, 'QO' will come in place of question mark. Hence, option (a) is correct.

10. *(d)* As, C = Cat (3 letters)

Similarly, N = $\boxed{Net}$ (3 letters)

So, 'Net' will come in place of question mark. Hence, option (d) is correct.

11. *(d)* As, P   Q $\boxed{R}$

Next   Next

Similarly,   D   E $\boxed{F}$

Next   Next

So, F is the missing letter.

12. (c) As, $\underset{F}{6} \xrightarrow{+2} \underset{H}{8}$ Similarly, $\underset{U}{21} \xrightarrow{+2} \underset{W}{23}$

$\underset{G}{7} \xrightarrow{+2} \underset{I}{9}$ $\underset{V}{22} \xrightarrow{+2} \underset{X}{24}$

So, the missing letters are 'WX'.

13. *(a)* As, T U V : W X Y
$+1$ $+1$ $+1$ $+1$ $+1$

Similarly, I J K : $\boxed{L\ M\ N}$
$+1$ $+1$ $+1$ $+1$ $+1$

So, the missing letters are 'LMN'.

14. (c) As, $\underset{6}{F} \xrightarrow{+1} \underset{7}{G}$

Similarly, $\underset{12}{F} \xrightarrow{+1} \underset{13}{M}$

15. *(b)* As, the sun shines during the day. Similarly , moon shines during the night.

16. *(d)* As, tongue is used to taste the food. Similarly, ears are used to hear the sound.

17. *(a)* As, bird flies in the sky. Similarly, duck swims in the water.

18. *(d)* The pattern is as follows :

As, C $\longrightarrow$ Three (position of C in English alphabetical series in forward direction)
+2 $\downarrow$
E $\longrightarrow$ Five (position of E in English alphabetical series in forward direction)

Similarly, I $\longrightarrow$ Nine (position of I in English alphabetical series in forward direction)
+2 $\downarrow$
K $\longrightarrow$ Eleven (position of K in English alphabetical series in forward direction)

So, K-Eleven should come in place of question mark.

19. *(c)* As, triangle has three sides. Similarly, the square has four sides.

20. (d) Mango is a fruit as brinjal is a vegetable.

2. Odd One Out

1. *(b)* Except dog all are birds.

2. *(d)* Except the clock in option (d), the hands in all the clocks are in straight line.

3. *(c)* In all the options (a), (b) and (d) sparrow is standing, while in option (c) it is sitting down.

4. *(c)* Figure in option (c) i.e. circle is different from other figures because they are made up of lines.

5. *(d)* In all the figures except option (d), both the shapes are on opposite sides to each other, while in option (d), the shapes are on the same side.

6. *(c)* All the figures except figure in option (c) are having same number of elements inside the main figure. So, figure (c) is different from others.

7. *(c)* Except option (c), in all others options, numbers of (#) inside the shapes is equal to the number of lines required to make the figure.

8. *(d)* All others except option (d) have been divided vertically.

9. *(b)* Except bat with number 13, all other bats are having even number, whereas bat '13' is an odd number bat. So, it is different from others.

10. *(b)* Except 809, all other numbers are divisible by 3. So, 809 does not belong the group.

11. *(c)* Except 14, all other numbers are prime numbers. So, 14 is different in the group.

12. (c) As, $8 \times 3 = 24$
$4 \times 6 = 24$
$12 \times 2 = 24$
but, $9 \times 7 = 63$
Except option (c), product of all others is same.

13. *(d)* As, $16 \div 4 = 4$
$32 \div 8 = 4$
$28 \div 7 = 4$
but, $25 \div 5 = 5$
Except option (d), Quotient of all others is same.

14. *(c)* Except letter 'E', all others are made up of three lines, whereas letter 'E' is made up of four lines.

15. *(d)* The pattern in the group of letters is as follows :

F $\longleftarrow$ D, M $\longleftarrow$ K, V $\longleftarrow$ T
$\quad$ E $\qquad$ L $\qquad$ U
But, R $\longleftarrow$ O
$\quad$ Q, P
So, 'RO' does not belong to the group.

16. *(d)* In the group of letters except in option (d), first and last letters are same. While, option (d) is different.

17. (b) As, $\overset{5}{E} \overset{+1}{\longrightarrow} \overset{6}{F}$; $\overset{12}{L} \overset{+1}{\longrightarrow} \overset{13}{M}$; $\overset{15}{O} \overset{+1}{\longrightarrow} \overset{16}{P}$
But, $\overset{7}{G} \overset{+3}{\longrightarrow} \overset{10}{J}$
So, GJ is different from others.

18. *(a)* As, H $\quad$ I $\quad$ J ; W $\quad$ X $\quad$ Y
$\quad \overset{}{\underset{+1}{\llcorner}} \overset{}{\underset{+1}{\lrcorner}} \quad \overset{}{\underset{+1}{\llcorner}} \overset{}{\underset{+1}{\lrcorner}}$
L $\quad$ M $\quad$ N ; P $\quad$ Q $\quad$ P
$\quad \overset{}{\underset{+1}{\llcorner}} \overset{}{\underset{+1}{\lrcorner}} \quad \overset{}{\underset{+1}{\llcorner}} \overset{}{\underset{+1}{\lrcorner}}$
So, PQP is different from others.

19. *(c)* Except truck, all others are electronics items.

3. What Comes Next?

1. *(a)* Elements in the first and third balloons are same. Elements in the second and fourth balloons are same. So, the next balloon will be same as first and third. Hence, option (a) is correct.

2. *(c)* First and fifth dolls are same. So, the sixth doll should be same as the second doll, as given in option (c).

3. *(b)* First and fifth figures are same. So, the second and sixth figures must be same. Therefore the next figure will be as shown in option (b).

4. *(a)* In pattern 1st, there are 3 teddies; in pattern 2nd, there are 6 teddies and in pattern 3rd, there are 9 teddies.

So, the pattern is as follows :

$$3 \xrightarrow{+3} 6 \xrightarrow{+3} 9 \xrightarrow{+3} 12 \xrightarrow{+3} \boxed{15}$$

Thus, there should be 15 teddies in pattern 5.

5. *(b)* The water in the glass decreases gradually in every successive glass. So, the next glass should be as shown in option (b).

6. *(c)* The squares in the circle increase by two in every next figure. So, there should be eight squares in the last figure as shown in option figure (c).

7. *(a)* In pattern Ist, there are 2 lollipop; in pattern 2nd there are 3 lollipop and in pattern 3rd, there are 4 lollipop. So, the pattern is as follows:

$$2 \xrightarrow{+1} 3 \xrightarrow{+1} 4 \xrightarrow{+1} 5 \xrightarrow{+1} \boxed{6}$$

Thus, there should be 6 lollpop in pattern 5.

8. *(b)* The pattern is as follows :

$$6 \xrightarrow{+6} 12 \xrightarrow{+6} 18 \xrightarrow{+6} 24$$

So, '24' will continue the series.

9. *(a)* The pattern is as follows :

Ist series, $2 \xrightarrow{+1} 3 \xrightarrow{+1} 4 \xrightarrow{+1} 5$

IInd series, $2 \xrightarrow{+1} 3 \xrightarrow{+1} 4 \xrightarrow{+1} 5$

IIIrd series, $3 \xrightarrow{+1} 4 \xrightarrow{+1} 5 \xrightarrow{+1} 6$

So, '556' is the missing number.

10. *(b)* The pattern is as follows :

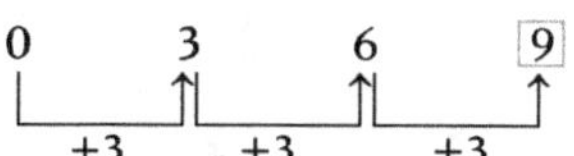

So, 9 will continue the series.

11. *(b)* The pattern is as follows :

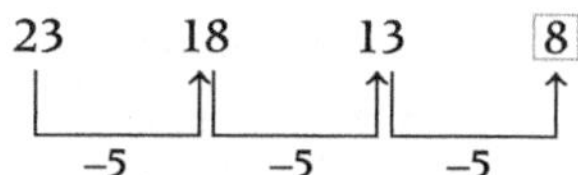

So, '8' will continue the series.

12. *(d)* The pattern is as follows :

So, '16' will continue the series.

13. *(d)* The pattern is as follows :

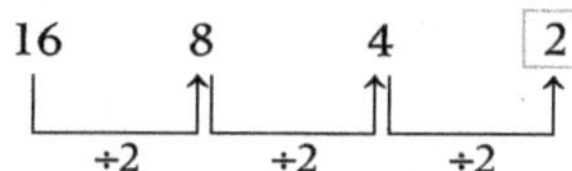

So, '2' will continue the series.

14. *(b)* The Pattern is as follows :

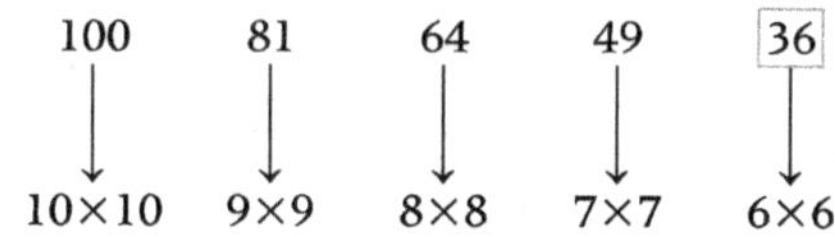

So, 36 will replace the question mark.

15. *(c)* The pattern is as follows :

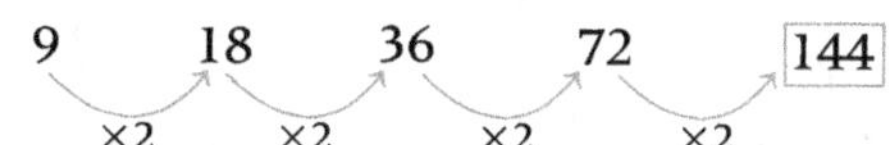

So, '144' is the missing number.

16. *(a)* The pattern is as follows :

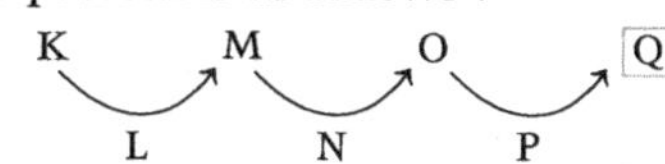

So, 'Q' will be on the last paper held by the girl.

17. *(d)* The pattern is as follows :

Ist series, $M \xrightarrow{+1} N \xrightarrow{+1} O \xrightarrow{+1} \boxed{P}$

IInd series, $D \xrightarrow{+1} E \xrightarrow{+1} F \xrightarrow{+1} \boxed{G}$

So, 'PG' will continue the series of letters.

18. *(a)* The pattern is as follows :

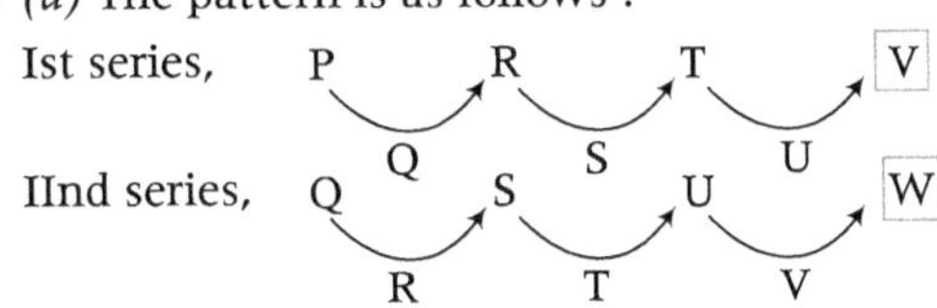

So, 'VW' will continue the series.

19. (b) The pattern is as follows :

Ist series,   G ⟶ H ⟶ I ⟶ J ⟶ [K]

IInd series,   B ⟶ C ⟶ D ⟶ E ⟶ [F]

So, KF is the next pair of letters.

20. (a) The pattern is as follows :

Ist series,   Q —PO→ N —ML→ K —JI→ [H]

IInd series,   L —M→ N —O→ P —Q→ [R]

So, HR is the next pair of letters.

21. (b) The middle letters which are vowels have an increasing trend of A, E, I, O, U and remaining letters have been retained as it is. So, answer would be TUF.

22. (b) The pattern is as follows :

Ist series,   J —+1→ K —+1→ L —+1→ [M]

IInd series,   A —+1→ B —+1→ C —+1→ [D]

IIIrd series,   S —+1→ T —+1→ U —+1→ [V]

IVth series,   U —+1→ V —+1→ W —+1→ [X]

So, 'M D V X' will continue the series.

4. Coding-Decoding

1. (c) The code of 🍾 is 'B' and the code of 🥛 is 'G'.

So, the code of 🍾🥛 is 'BG'.

2. (a) The code of 🚗 is 'T' and the code of 🏁🏁 is 'F'.

So, the code of 🚗 🏁🏁 is 'TF'.

3. (d) The code of 🚲 is 'C' and the code of 🧍 is 'M'.

So, the code of 🚲 🧍 is 'CM'.

4. (b) The codes of letters are as follow :
P → e, A → 2, R → #, E → 4, N → l, T → $
So, the code of 'PARENT' is 'e2#41$'.

5. (d) The codes of letters are as follow :
C → 0, O → ◎, U → 8, N → l, T → $
So, the code of 'COUNT' is '0◎81$'.

6. (b) The codes of numbers are as follows :
3 → ×, 4 → ÷, 2 → −, 5 → +
So, the code of 3425 is × ÷ − +

7. (a) The colour of sky at night is Black, but here Black is called Green.
So, the colour of sky is Green at night.

8. (a) A person will sit on 'chair' but a 'chair' is called roof. So, a person will sit on the roof.

9. (b) Cricket is played with a bat and bat is called racket. So, cricket is played with a 'racket'.

10. (c) The ring's shape is ◯, but here ◯ is called ▢.
So, the geometrical shape ▢ is ring.

11. (c) 🛵 is a two wheeler vehicle, but here 🛵 is called 🚚 .
So, 🚚 is a two wheeler vehicle.

12. (a) As,

R E E H C
↘ ↗ ↑ ↖ ↙
C H E E R

Similarly,

[R I A H C]
↘ ↗ ↑ ↖ ↙
C H A I R

and Y E K N O M
↙ ↖ ↑ ↗ ↘
M O N K E Y

So, 'RIAHC' is the code for 'CHAIR'.

13. (a) As,

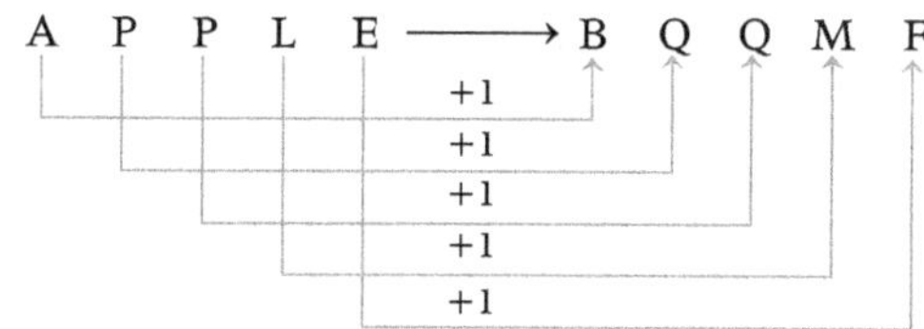

Similarly,

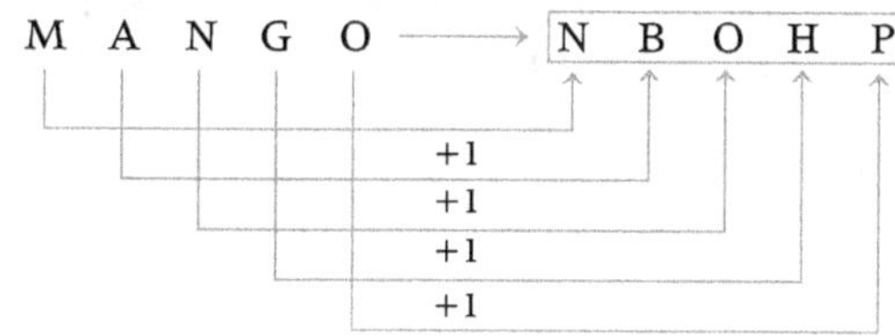

14. (d) Each word is coded by the numeral which is equal the number of letters in the word. Since, there are 8 letters in the given word ABHISHEK. So, required code is 8.

15. (d) As,

R	A	M	A	N
4	5	6	5	2

and

C	H	A	M	A	N
3	1	5	6	5	2

Similarly,

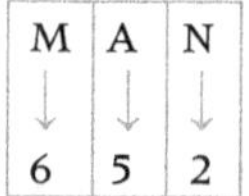

M	A	N
6	5	2

So, '652' is the code for 'MAN'.

5. Alphabet and Word Formation Test

1. (c) 'E' will end the first word 'ONE' and start the second word 'EAT'.

2. (d) 'L' will end the first word 'MALL' and start the second word 'LAKE'.

3. (b) Letter 'I' when replaced with question mark will make the name of fruit KIWI and name of vegetable TURNIP.

4. (d) Letter 'D' should be replaced with question mark to make the name of two amphibians CROCODILE and TADPOLE.

5. (a) The word formed after arranging the given letters is ORANGE, which is a fruit.

6. (c) The word formed after arranging the given letters is 'CRICKET', which is a sport.

7. (b) Considering option (b);

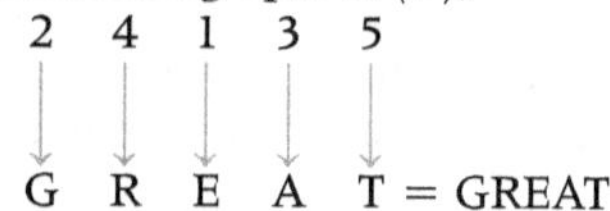

So, after arranging the number '24135', we get a meaningful word 'GREAT'. Hence, option (b) is correct.

8. (d) Considering option (d);

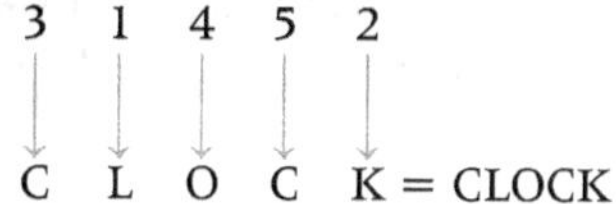

So, after arranging the numbers '31452', we get a meaningful word 'CLOCK'. Hence, option (d) is correct.

9. (c) Considering option (c);

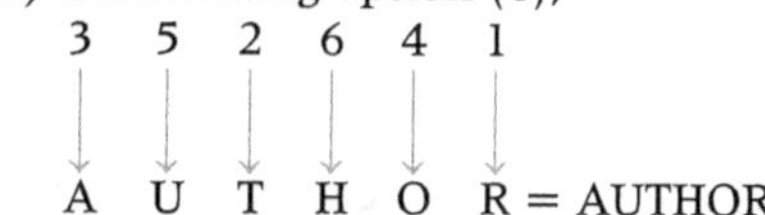

So, after arranging the numbers '352641', we get a meaningful word 'AUTHOR'. Hence, option (c) is correct.

10. (c) Considering option (c);

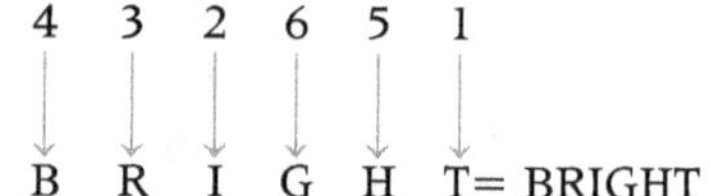

So, after arranging the numbers '432651', we get a meaningful word 'BRIGHT'. Hence option (c) is correct.

11. (c) The word 'MIND' can be formed using the letters of the given word EXAMINED.

12. (d) The word 'GOAL' can be formed using the letters of the given word LOGICAL.

13. (d) The word 'ANIMATION' can be formed using the letters of the given word 'EXAMINATION'.

14. (d) The word 'MAGIC' can be formed using the letters of the given word 'PRAGMATIC'.

15. (c) The word 'GAME' cannot be formed using the letters of the given word LAUGHTER.

16. (c) The word 'NICE' cannot be formed using the letters of the given word 'NECESSARY'.

17. *(a)* Considering option (a),

So, number of letters between adjacent letters is same. Hence option (a) is correct.

18. *(b)* Considering option (b).

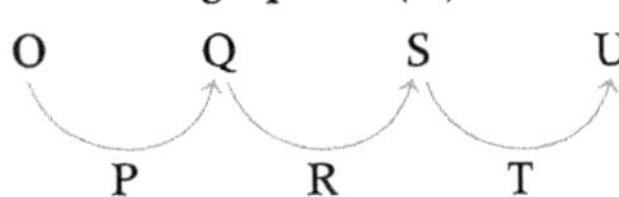

So, number of letter skipped between adjacent letters is same. Hence option (b) is correct.

6. Complete the Figure

1. *(c)* The pattern can be completed by using the figure in option (c).

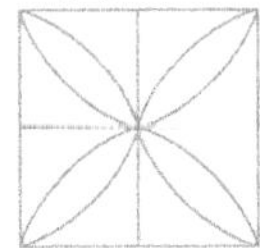

2. *(d)* The given pattern can be completed by using the figure in option (d).

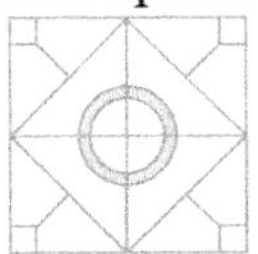

3. *(c)* The pattern can be completed by using the figure in option (c).

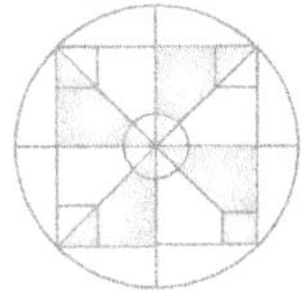

4. *(b)* The pattern can be completed by using the figure in option (b).

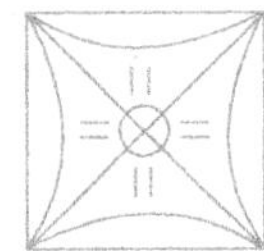

5. *(c)* The pattern can be completed by using the figure in option (c).

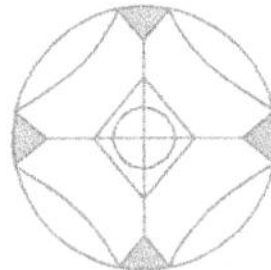

6. *(d)* The given pattern can be completed by using the figure in option (d).

7. *(c)* The pattern can be completed by using the figure in option (c).

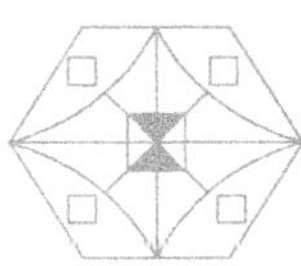

8. *(d)* The pattern can be completed by using the figure in option (d).

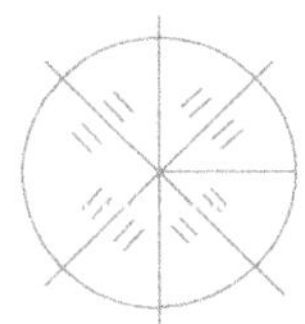

9. *(b)* The pattern can be completed by using the figure in option (b).

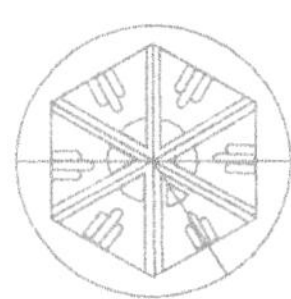

10. *(a)* The pattern can be completed by using the figure in option (a).

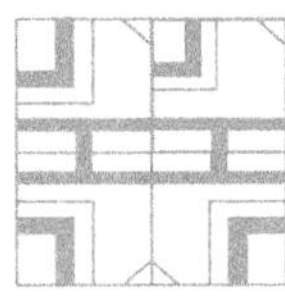

7. Hidden Figures

1. *(b)* The given shape is hidden in the picture in option (b) as shown in given below.

2. (*a*) The given shape is hidden in the figure in option (a) as shown in given below.

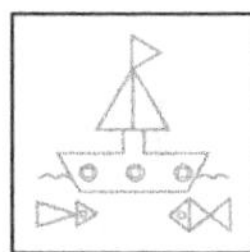

3. (*b*) The same part shown in figure (X) belongs to the toy picture in option (b) as shown in given below.

4. (*b*) The given shape is hidden in the figure in option (b) as shown in given below.

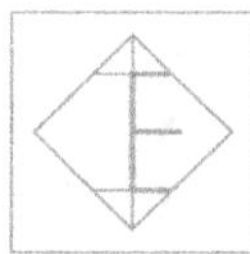

5. (*b*) The given shape is hidden in the figure in option (b) as shown in given below.

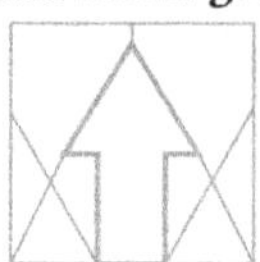

6. (*c*) The given shape is hidden in option figure (c) as shown in given below.

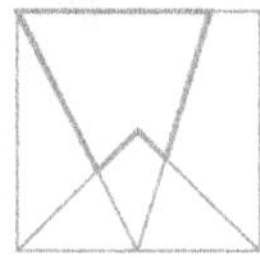

7. (*d*) The given shape is hidden in the figure in option (d) as shown in given below.

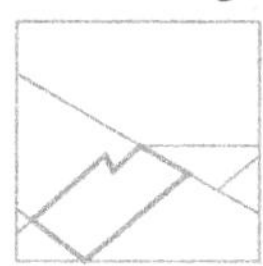

8. (*b*) The given part belongs to the figure in option (b) as shown in given below.

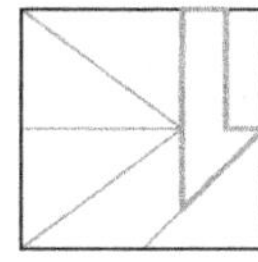

9. (*d*) Figure in option (d) is hidden in triangle shaped pattern as shown in given below.

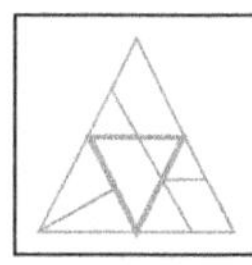

10. (*d*) Figure in option (d) is hidden in the given figure (X) as shown in given below.

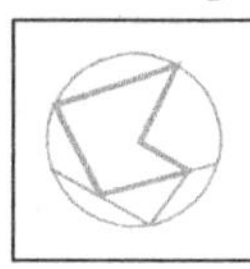

11. (*a*) Figure in option (a) is hidden in the given figure (X) as shown in given below.

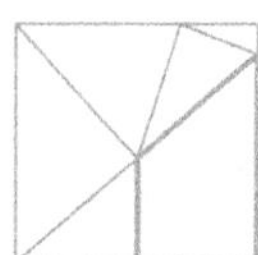

12. (*c*) Figure in option (c) is hidden in the given figure (X) as shown in given below.

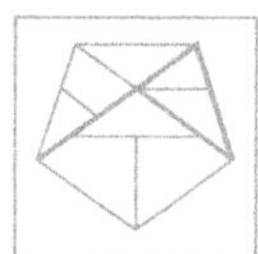

13. (*c*) In option (c) figure, specified components of figure (X) are found.

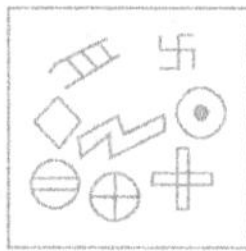

14. (*b*) Figure in option (b) is hidden in the given figure (X) as shown in given below.

15. (*c*)

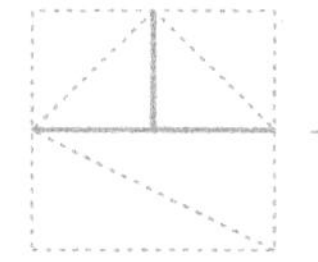

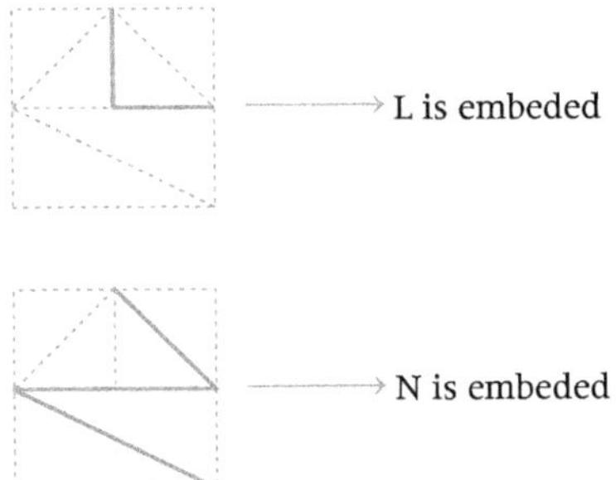

So, M is NOT embedded in the given figure (X).

16. (c) Option (c) figure 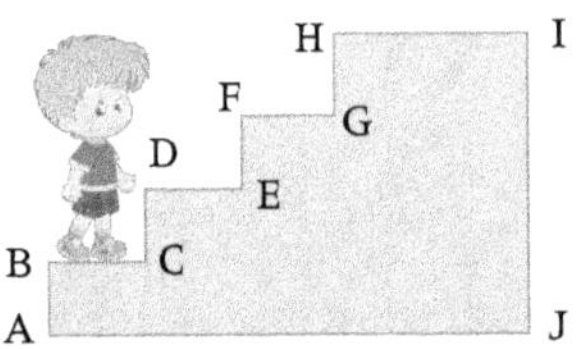 is NOT embedded in the given figure (X).

17. (b) Option (b) figure 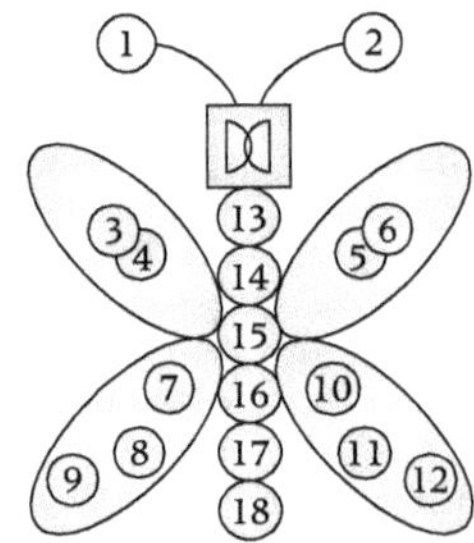 is NOT embedded in the given figure (X).

8. Counting of Figures

1. (c) The given picture can be labelled as shown below :

Number of straight lines = AB, BC, CD, DE, EF, FG, GH, HI, IJ, AJ = 10

2. (b) There are four different closed shapes in the given picture which are circle, triangle, square and rectangle.

3. (b) The given picture can be labelled as shown below :

So, there are 18 circles in the given picture.

4. (c) The picture can be labelled as shown below

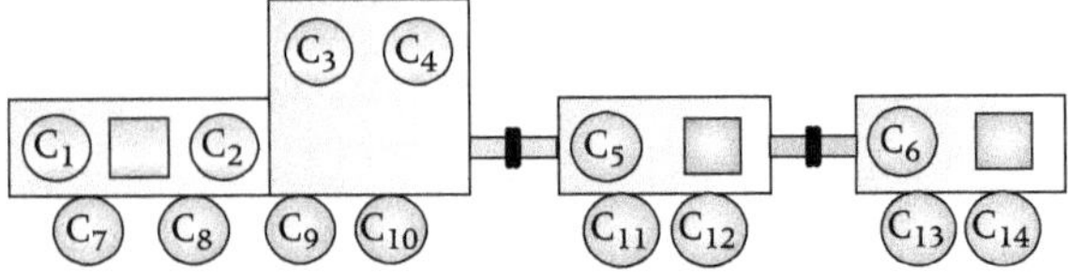

So, the number of circles in the above picture is 14.

5. (c) The picture can be labelled as shown below

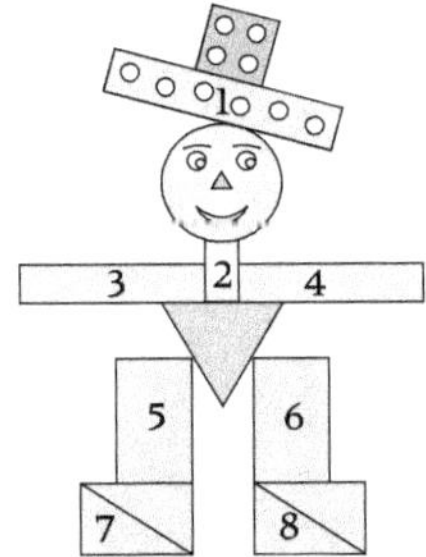

So, there are 8 rectangles in the given picture.

6. (a) The given shape of kite can be labelled as shown below :

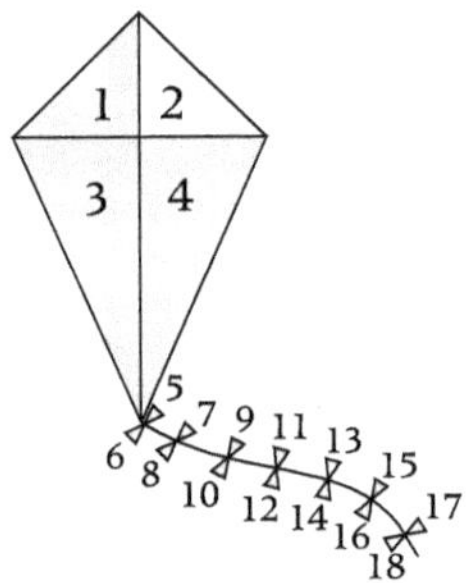

Number of triangles as they are labelled are 18 in numbers, but there are four more triangles which are formed by combining 1 and 2, 3 and 4, 1 So, 3 and 2 and 4.

∴ So, total number of triangles = 18 + 4 = 22

7. (a) The picture can be labelled as shown below:

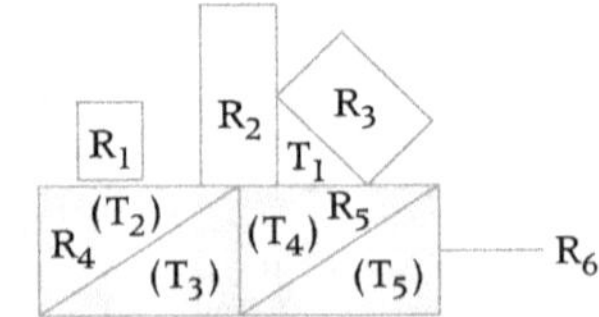

So, there are six rectangles and five triangles.

8. *(d)* The number of slant lines in the given picture of X-mas tree can be shown as :

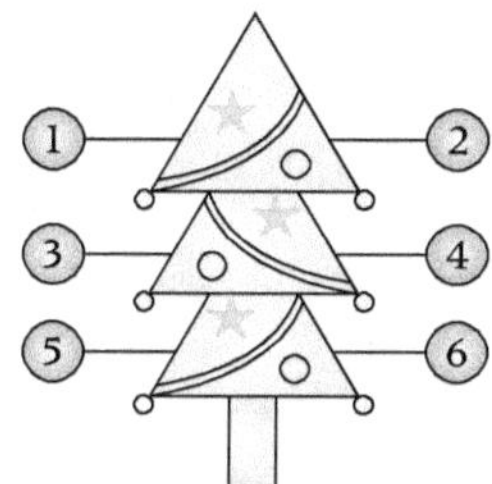

So, there are six slant lines as we count.

9. *(d)* In the given picture four different shapes are there which are circle, star, triangle and rectangle.

10. *(a)* The given image can be labelled as shown below :

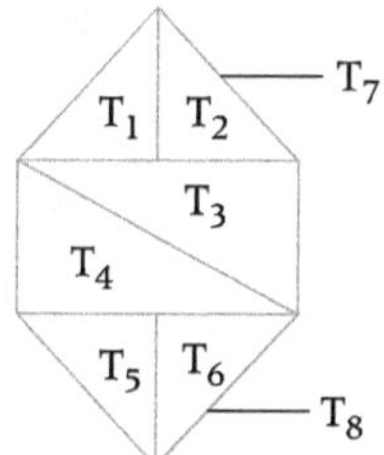

So, there are 8 triangles in the given image.

11. *(b)* The given image can be labelled as shown below :

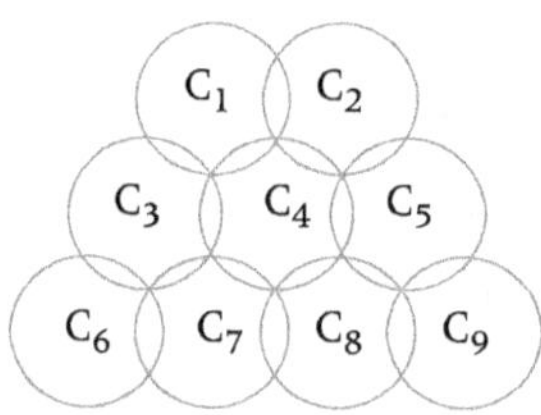

So, there are 9 circles in the given image.

12. *(c)* The given image can be labelled as shown below :

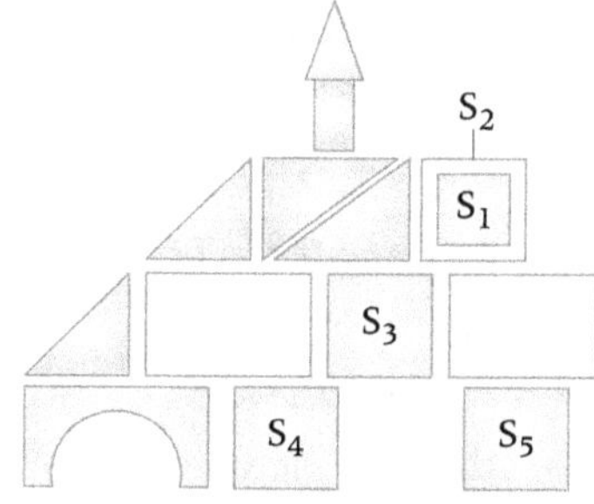

So, there are 5 squares in the given image

13. *(a)* The given image can be labelled as shown below :

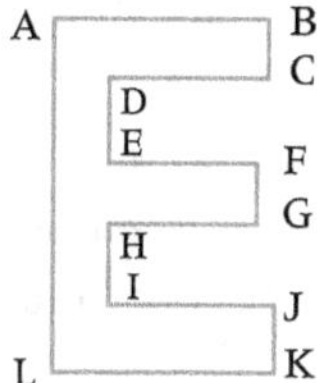

Number of straight line = AB, BC, CD, DE, EF, FG, GH, HI, IJ, JK, KL, LA = 12

Sol. (Q. Nos. 14 and 15) The given picture can be labelled as shown below.

14. *(b)* Number of triangles in the given picture is 13 when they are counted.

15. *(a)* Number of triangles = 13
and number of circles = 11
So, required difference = 13 − 11 = 2

9. Grouping of Figures

1. *(a)* Each row must have one $\triangle$, one $\triangle$ and one $\triangle$. So, the missing shape in second row is $\triangle$.

2. *(d)* In each row, after joining the first and second firgure we get the third figure. So, option (d) figure will come in place of question mark. Hence, option (d) is correct.

3. *(d)* There are three shaded figures; a circle, a triangle and a square. Each row and each column contains a circle, a square and a triangle at different positions. So, the missing figure should be ⊖.

4. (*d*) In each row, after joining the first and third figure, we get the second figure, so option (d) will come in place of question mark. Hence option (d) is correct.

5. (*c*) All elements are the multiple of 2, so option (c) will replace the question mark. Hence, option (c) is correct.

6. (*a*) Considering option (a); Figures 1, 5, 7 are composed of triangle.

   Figures 3, 4, 9 are composed of circle.

   and Figures 2, 6, 8 are composed of rectangle.

   Hence, option (a) is correct.

7. (*c*) Considering option (c); Figures 1, 5, 8 two different elements intersecting each other.

   Figures 2, 3, 9 two similar elements intersecting each other.

   Figures 4, 6, 7 two different elements one placed inside the other.

   Hence, option (c) is correct.

8. (*c*) Considering option (c),

   Figures 1, 2, 4 consists one shape.

   Figures 3, 5, 7 consists two shapes.

   and figures 6, 8, 9 consists three

   Hence option (c) is correct.

9. (*a*) Considering option (a)

   Numbers 1, 3, 9 equals to 2.

   Numbers 2, 6, 7 equals to 5.

   and Numbers 4, 5, 8 equals to 3

   Hence option (a) is correct.

10. (*b*) In above 15 mangoes, group of 5 mangoes is shown below :

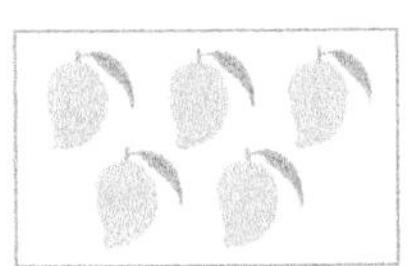 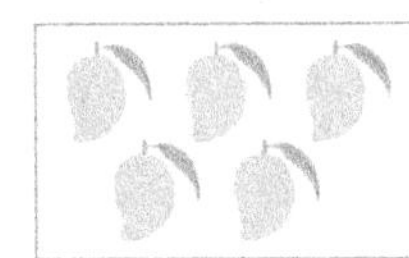

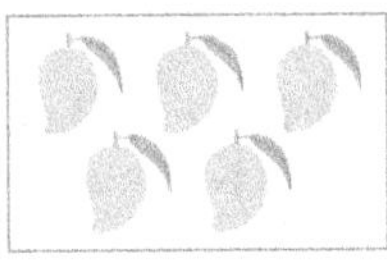

So, 3 groups of 5 mangoes can be formed from given mangoes.

10. Mirror Images

1. (*b*)   2. (*b*)   3. (*d*)

4. (*b*)   5. (*d*)   6. (*d*)

7. (*c*)   8. (*b*)   9. (*c*)

10. (*c*)

11. Position and Comparison Test

1. (*b*) The positions of the toys hanging in a toy shop can be shown as :

   Left A B C D E F G H I J K L Right

   5th to the left

   So, D is 5th to the left of toy I.

2. (*c*) The arrangement of the books can be shown as :

   Top

   K

   L   3rd from the top

   M

   N

   O   5th from the bottom

   P

   Q

   Bottom

   So, M is at 5th position from the bottom.

3. (*b*) The given letters shown below :

   Left O X Q A E D G L W R Y Right

   5th to the right

   So, G is 5th letter from the right end.

Sol. (Q. Nos. 4 and 5)

4. (*b*) Tree S is between tree R and tree T and this can be seen from the given arrangements as

   R S T

5. (*c*) The arrangement can be shown as :

   P Q R S T U V

   Left   4th to the right   Right

   So, U is 4th to the right of tree Q.

6. (*b*) The positions of teddies after interchanging can be shown as :

D E J G [H] I F K

Left   Right
                2nd to the left

So, H is second to the left of F when F and J interchange their positions.

Sol. (Q. Nos. 7 and 8)

7. (*c*) The position of the boys can be shown as :

5 boys

Left 1 ② 3 4 5 6 7 ⑧ 9 10 Right

So, there are 5 boys between the boys on 2nd and 8th position.

8. (*c*) After interchanging the positions the arrangement is shown as :

Left 1 8 3 4 ⑤ 6 7 2 9 10 Right
                → 3rd to the right

So, boy at 5th position is third to the right of 8th boy after interchanging the positions.

Sol. (Q. Nos. 9 and 10)

9. (*b*) The arrangement of teddies can be shown as

Left A B [C] D E F G Right

5th to the right

As, we can see from the arrangement, teddy C is at 5th position from the right end.

10. (*d*) When teddy F is removed from the row, then teddy E is to the immediate left of teddy G, which can be shown as :

Left A B C D [E] F̶ G Right

Immediate left

11. (*c*) The arrangement after the removal of flowers can be shown as :

③

Left 1 2 3 4 5 6 7 8 9̶ 10 Right

So, there are three flowers between 5th and 10th flower.

Sol. (Q. Nos. 12 and 13)

12. (*a*) The arrangement of the ice-cream cones in the stand can be shown as :

Left E F G H I J K L M N Right

⑤

So, it is clear that there are 5 ice-cream cones to the left of cone J.

13. (*d*) The arrangement of the ice-cream cones after the removal of cones G and M can be shown as :

E F G H [I] J K L M̶

As, we can see the arrangement of cone I is in the middle of the stand.

14. (*b*) The arrangement of bats can be shown as

Left T U [V] W X Y Z Right

3rd to the left

So, Bat V is at third position from the left end.

15. (*c*) The arrangement of bats can be shown as

Left T U V W X Y Z Right

As, we can see the arrangement, Bat X is in the middle of W and Y.

16. (*b*) The arrangement of students according to the marks scored by them can be shown as :

Harry > Peter > Bob > Andy

From the above arrangement, it is clear that Harry scored the highest marks.

[here, '>' symbol is used to show more than]

12. Find Direction

1. (*a*) The directions of the places can be shown as

House (North)

Grocery shop   Centre   Church (East)
(West)
               Temple (South)

So, it is clear that house is in the North direction from the Temple.

2. (*c*) The place which is in the West direction can be shown as :

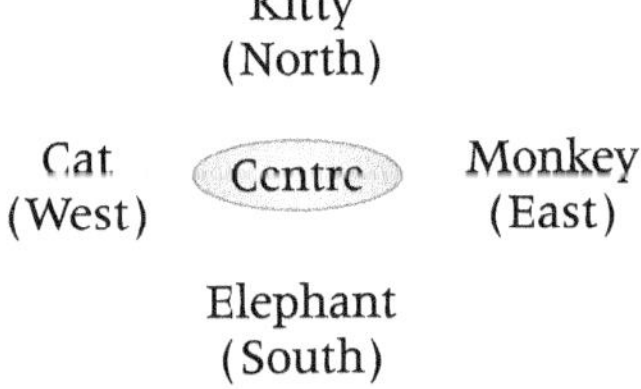

So, it is clear that grocery shop is in the West direction.

3. (*b*) The directions of the toys in which they are kept can be shown as :

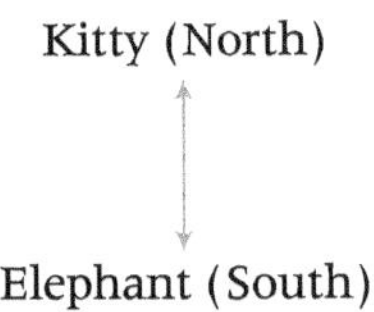

So, it is clear from above that cat is in the West direction from the monkey.

4. (*a*) The toy which is in the North direction can be shown as :

Kitty (North)
↑
↓
Elephant (South)

So, from above it is clear that Kitty is in the North direction.

5. (*d*) The item which is in the West direction can be shown as :

Cock (West) ← → Fruits basket (East)

So, it is clear that cock is in West direction.

6. (*a*) The directions of items can be shown as :

Clock (North)
Cock (West)   Centre   Fruits basket (East)
Briefcase (South)

So, it is clear from above that clock is in the North direction from the briefcase.

Sol. (Q. Nos. 7 and 8) The directions in the map of India can be shown as :

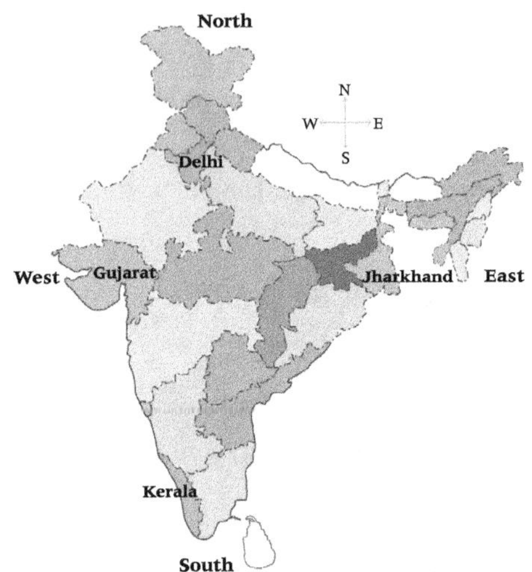

7. (*d*) It is clear from the above map of India, Kerala is in the South direction.

8. (*a*) Gujarat is in the West direction from Jharkhand as shown in the above map.

9. (*c*) The direction in which Martin is standing can be shown as :

Tom (North)
Harry (West)   Centre   Julia (East)
Martin (South)

So, it is clear from above that Martin is standing in South direction.

10. (*b*) The person standing in the East direction can be shown as :

Harry (West) ← → Julia (East)

So, Julia is standing in the East direction.

11. (*b*) The train which is in the East direction can be shown as :

Train C (West) ← → Train B (East)

So, it is clear that Train B is in East direction.

12. (*b*) The directions of trains can be shown as

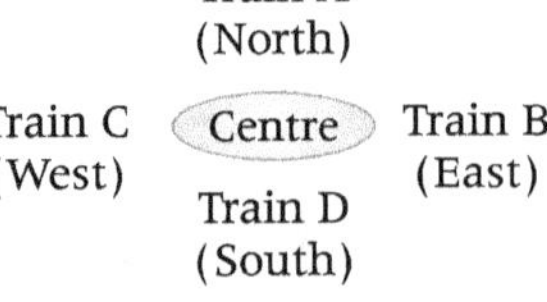

So, it is clear that Train A is in the North direction.